The Networked Library

The Networked Library

A Guide for the Educational Use of Social Networking Sites

MELISSA A. PURCELL

TECH TOOLS FOR LEARNING

LINWORTH

AN IMPRINT OF ABC-CLIO, LLC
Santa Barbara, California • Denver, Colorado • Oxford, England

Library of Congress Cataloging-in-Publication Data

Purcell, Melissa A.

The networked library : a guide for the educational use of social networking sites / Melissa A. Purcell.

pages cm.—(Tech tools for learning)

Includes bibliographical references and index.

ISBN 978-1-58683-545-3 (pbk.)—ISBN 978-1-58683-546-0 (ebook) 1. Internet in school libraries. 2. Online social networks—Library applications. 3. Internet in education. 4. Online social networks. 5. Social media. 6. Electronic information resource literacy—Study and teaching (Elementary)—Activity programs. 7. Electronic information resource literacy—Study and teaching (Secondary)—Activity programs. 8. School librarian participation in curriculum planning. 9. Education—Curricula— Standards—United States. I. Title.

Z675.S3P86 2012

302.30285—dc23   2012007370

ISBN: 978-1-58683-545-3
EISBN: 978-1-58683-546-0

16 15 14 13 12   1 2 3 4 5

This book is also available on the World Wide Web as an eBook.
Visit www.abc-clio.com for details.

Linworth
An Imprint of ABC-CLIO, LLC

ABC-CLIO, LLC
130 Cremona Drive, P.O. Box 1911
Santa Barbara, California 93116-1911

This book is printed on acid-free paper ∞

Manufactured in the United States of America

All Common Core State Standards © 2010. National Governors Association Center for Best Practices and Council of Chief State School Officers. All rights reserved.

All National Educational Technology Standards for Students, Second Edition © 2007. ISTE® (International Society for Technology in Education), www.iste.org. All rights reserved.

*I dedicate this book to
Jason and Jesse,
who form the best social network
I am a member of.*

Contents

Acknowledgments

I would like to thank my family, who made personal sacrifices to allow me the time needed to complete this book.

   I would like to thank Dr. Judi Repman, who not only edited the book and encouraged me to write the book in the first place, but who has been a constant friend and mentor in my life for the last six years.

Introduction

Social networking sites are part of our students' daily lives, and they are experts in using them. Students are enthusiastic about using social networking, and some students are spending more time on these sites than in school—over 40 hours a week according to some students I surveyed. Although networking sites are used by many students and teachers alike, introducing online networking concepts into the classroom is a novel idea to many educators. Many students walk around campuses with phones that can connect to the Internet so they are never far from their beloved networking communities. In our society, we now feel stranded on a deserted island in the middle of nowhere if the battery in our mobile device unexpectedly dies and leaves us out of touch from our networks for any period of time.

Learning has a social context, and we must embrace that fact. Teachers need to try to incorporate their students' current knowledge and passion for networking sites into their classroom learning experiences or the sites will still be used but as a distraction instead of a learning experience. Teachers may be so overwhelmed with daily lesson plans, testing, meetings, student discipline, and so forth that they may not be eager to incorporate another project or new technologies into their already hectic schedules. Teachers may wonder how they are supposed to fit in one more thing with everything else they are already juggling. The thought of taking on one more task often has teachers wanting to run screaming in the opposite direction. This is where librarians step in and help alleviate the anxiety associated with integrating these valuable resources into the classroom. Librarians are the technology experts who can ensure that networking sites are effectively integrated into a school. Many librarians are also new to the use of networking sites, so this book will provide the foundation for building the skills needed to become a social networking expert.

School librarians should be experts in digital resources; librarians can help students use networking sites as well as offer professional development trainings for teachers in order to prepare them to implement networking site lessons with their students. When used educationally, networking sites can empower students to become content producers rather than content consumers by assigning them projects that require a product rather than the unproductive copy-and-paste projects that many teachers currently use. Networking can open a whole new world to students by facilitating collaborative learning opportunities. As you will read in chapter 1, the benefits of incorporating networking sites into the classroom are numerous.

Who Should Use This Book

This book will offer school librarians, teachers, school administrators, college professors, and public librarians the "why" and especially the "how to" information needed to effectively use networking tools to facilitate student learning and achievement. Today librarians and educators face the difficult task of keeping up with the latest technologies available on the Internet, keeping students motivated to learn, and knowing how to incorporate the latest technologies into the classroom setting to enhance learning. This book will help with all three of these problems.

Personal social networking sites encourage students to interact with each other, and using similar sites educationally will incorporate the same activities students already love but with an educational objective. Most educators do not know how to use networking technologies and tools for academic success and career readiness. If you are a librarian reading this book, you need to recruit teachers and administrators to incorporate these lesson plans and help unblock any existing filters. If you are a teacher or administrator, you need to work with the librarian to collaborate on these lessons. If you are a public librarian, all the communication and professional development information applies, but obviously lessons would just be enrichment activities for your patrons.

Author Blog

This book is full of reproducible documents used in lesson plans, rubrics to go along with those lesson plans, and handouts for patrons. All of the reproducible documents found in this book (along with additional resources that will be added after publication) will be available on my blog at http://networkedlibrary.wordpress.com/ (password "library"). Following is the QR code to take you directly to the blog.

> **QR code stands for "quick response barcode."** QR codes are two-dimensional barcodes that can be read by dedicated QR scanners or smartphones. These barcodes can encode URLs (uniform resource locators, more commonly known as Web addresses), text, phone numbers, and more. Free websites can be used to generate a QR code within seconds. This QR code was created by Quikqr (http://quikqr.com), a site that has both a QR code generator and a QR code reader. A QR code reader app must be installed on smartphones in order to actually scan the barcode.

Blog Content

To avoid having to restate that a document or resource is available on the blog every time one of the resources is discussed, Table I.1 lists the content for all the resources that can be found on the blog.

Reproducible rubrics are provided with every lesson in this book. Many educators consider rubrics to be limiting and refuse to use them to encourage more creativity from their students. These rubrics are not intended to be limiting but are supposed to provide a basic guideline for teachers and students to follow. These les-

TABLE I.1   List of Blog Resources

Chapter 1: What Are Networking Sites and Why Use Them?

List of Networking Sites to Know
No need to type in the long web addresses for the networking sites referred to in each chapter, just go to the list of sites for that chapter and follow the hyperlink to the site.

Chapter 2: Guidelines to Keep Your Students and Yourself Safe When Integrating Networking Sites in the Classroom

List of Sites Mentioned in the Chapter
Acceptable Use Policy Example
Responsible Use Contract Example
Additional Resources Worth Checking Out

Chapter 3: Media Sharing Sites in the Classroom

List of Networking Sites to Know
Promotional Book Poster Rubric
Glog Example Created on Glogster Edu
Glog Example
Book Glog Rubric
Book Review Storyboard/Script
Book Review Storyboard/Script Example
Book Review Storyboard/Script Rubric
Thirty-Second Book Trailer Example
Thirty-Second Book Trailer Rubric
Two-Minute YouTube Book Trailer Example
Two-Minute YouTube Book Trailer Rubric
Additional Resources Worth Checking Out

Chapter 4: Microblogs and Wikis in the Classroom

List of Networking Sites to Know
Historical Tweets Examples
Book Summary Handout
Book Summary on Paper Rubric
Book Summary Example
Book Summary on a Secure Wiki Rubric
Twitter Book Summary Rubric
Wiki-Style Book Review Poster Template
Wiki-Style Book Review Poster Example
Wiki-Style Book Review Poster Rubric
Wiki-Style Book Review Rubric
Podcast Example
Podcast Book Review Wiki Rubric
Additional Resources Worth Checking Out

Chapter 5: Social Networking Sites in the Classroom

List of Networking Sites to Know
Character Activity Summary on Paper Template
Character Activity Summary on Paper Rubric
Character Activity Summary Template to Edit on the Computer
Character Activity Summary Example
Activity Summary Word Cloud Example
Character Activity Summary Rubric
Character Facebook Status Update Rubric
Person Profile Summary Template on Paper
Person Profile Summary Template Rubric
Profile Template to Edit on the Computer
Example Profile Page of Poet Pablo Neruda
Profile Rubric
Facebook Profile Rubric
Additional Resources Worth Checking Out

Chapter 6: A Few Final Words

Educators Worth Checking Out

Appendix

Chapter 3 Instruction Sheets:

YouTube, Customizing a YouTube Channel, Glogster, Animoto, Creating a Video in Animoto, One True Media, Creating a Video in Animoto, , Creating a Video Using JayCut, and Creative Commons

Chapter 4 Instruction Sheets:

Twitter, Wordle, Tagxedo, PBworks, Wikispaces, Vocaroo, and Voki

Chapter 5 Instruction Sheets:

Facebook and Edmodo

sons are designed to be student centered to allow students' choices to increase creativity and allow the students to take ownership of their learning. All of these rubrics can be modified to accomplish this with your particular students.

Chapter Structure

Each chapter begins with a word cloud, created using the free website Wordle (http://www.wordle.net/), to show the dominant terms found in that chapter. A *word cloud* is a visual representation of text with more frequently used words appearing larger. The word cloud at the beginning of the chapter will provide a glimpse of the overall theme of the text that follows. If you have never used Wordle before, it is a wonderful Web 2.0 tool that is educationally worthy of incorporation into lesson plans. Following each word cloud is a brief introduction to the networking category addressed in that particular chapter, followed by definitions of terms referred to in the chapter, and then a description of each networking site referred to in the chapter. Each chapter ends with a list of suggestions for additional resources that are worth checking out.

Book Structure

Chapter 1 provides a basic introduction to networking sites and reasons to incorporate these sites into lesson plans. Chapter 1 also includes concise recommendations for getting started using networking tools and advice for improving your current usage. Chapter 2 offers guidelines for keeping students and yourself safe while using the Internet and networking sites. Chapters 3, 4, and 5 provide detailed lesson plans that incorporate networking sites and include reproducible documents that will help simplify the incorporation of these lessons into your daily teaching.

Throughout this book I will refer to both social and educational networking sites as "networking sites" in order to simplify the terminology. The only exception is in chapter 5, which focuses on the social aspect of networking sites, so I stress the word *social* in that chapter to distinguish that category. I have broken the plethora of networking sites down into three categories that this book will address: media sharing sites (including but not limited to YouTube, TeacherTube, Wikimedia Commons, and Flickr), microblogs and wikis (including but not limited to Wikispaces, PBworks, and Twitter), and social networking sites (including but not limited to Facebook, Ning, and Edmodo).

Chapter Categories

Of course, there are many categories, but to have a manageable number I chose the three shown in Table I.2. There is also some overlap between the three categories, but I placed each networking site in the category that seemed the most fitting. Each category is addressed in its own chapter so that you can chose which category you would like to start with and go directly to that chapter—chapter 3 covers media sharing sites, chapter 4 focuses on microblogs and wikis, and chapter 5 concentrates on social networking sites. This book can be used by educators at any grade level, but the lessons are mainly aimed at grades five to adult. Please note that some sites included in this book are limited to users aged 13 and older (such as Ning and YouTube).

TABLE I.2   Chapter Categories

Chapter 3: Media Sharing Sites	Chapter 4: Microblogs/wikis Sites	Chapter 5: Social Networking Sites
• Websites used to upload, organize, and share digital video files (examples include YouTube and TeacherTube)	• Blogs: online communication mediums that allow one-to-many interaction (examples include Blogger and Class Blogmeister)	• Websites that build online communities with the intent of building relationships among people with similar interests (examples include Myspace and Facebook)
• Websites used to upload, organize, and share digital image files (examples include Flickr and Wikimedia Commons)	• Microblogs: online communication mediums that allow short one-to-many communications while also encouraging feedback and two-way communication (examples include Twitter and Plurk)	
• Websites used to upload, organize, and share digital audio files (examples include Jamendo and Wikimedia Commons)	• Wikis: online communication mediums that allow many-to-many interaction (examples include Wikispaces and PBworks)	

Move through the Stages

Each of the three lesson plan chapters offers multiple lessons that anyone can implement immediately regardless of technology limitations or experience level. Each lesson addresses Common Core State Standards and can be adapted to fit multiple subjects and grade levels. This book will show you how you can meet Common Core State Standards using networking sites as part of your lessons. The lesson plans provided in this book are divided into three stages:

Stage one: Implement stage one lesson plans if your school or library has very limited access to technology, such as only one computer per classroom or library area. Stage one lessons may require computer use for demonstrations or examples but do not require student use of technology. Since stage one lessons do not have students actually using the networking sites themselves, they are considered a stepping stone for introducing students to the technology in preparation for moving to stages two and three in the future. Stage one lessons are the least green of all the lesson stages because they require students to use paper products, such as poster board and notebook paper, in addition to other supplies. Stage one lessons have a limited audience because the finished product will usually only be seen in a library or single classroom unless posted in a prominent place in a school for others to see as they walk by. The stage one lessons mimic Web 2.0 technologies without actually using them so that students without access to those technologies can still be introduced to these concepts. Stage one lessons still build learning communities, but those communities only exist in their classroom and school instead of on the World Wide Web.

Stage two: Stage two lessons offer a medium ground between stage one lessons and stage three lessons by putting students online but in a secure community environment. Implement stage two lesson plans if your school or library has limited access to technology such as having a limited schedule for computer lab time or having a filter that limits access to specific Internet sites. Stage two lessons have students using computers and online resources that offer secure educational settings. Stage two lessons do not require students to actually use public networking sites that they are familiar with, so this stage is considered a stepping stone for preparing students to move on to stage three. Stage two is a greener stage than stage one if the teacher can grade the assignments online by: 1) posting to a wiki or school website (so all can see), 2) receiving the assignment through email, or 3) having the students save the assignment in a homework drive on the Intranet. Stage two lessons have a limited audience because the final products will usually only be seen by a single class or other limited audience within a school.

Stage three: Stage three lessons represent the pinnacle of the networked classroom. Implement stage three lesson plans if your school or library has ample access to technology. You will be able to implement stage three lessons if your school has one-to-one computing (every student has his/her own laptop every day) or you can take a whole class to a computer lab many times a week and filters do not limit access to Internet sites. Stage three lessons require students to use the networking sites they are familiar with (Facebook, Twitter, YouTube, etc.) to complete the lesson. Stage three lessons are the most green of all the lessons because the entire lesson is completed online, thus saving paper and other resources. Stage three lessons give students a huge authentic audience because they can be viewed by the entire world via the World Wide Web.

This is a practical book that educators can pick up and begin using today to move through the three stages.

Standards Provide a Learning Objective and Common Language

Each lesson plan includes reference to the Common Core State Standards that it addresses. The Common Core State Standards define the knowledge and skills students should have within their K–12 education careers so that they will graduate high school able to succeed in academic college courses and in workforce training programs. The Common Core State Standards will eventually be present in all the states.

For those unfamiliar with how the states came to adopt Common Core State Standards, here is a very brief history. In 1983, the publication of *A Nation at Risk: The Imperative for Educational Reform* set off an educational reform movement in the United States. Between 1983 and 1985 alone, over 700 pieces of educational reform legislation were enacted by the states in order to reform the educational system. In response to *A Nation at Risk,* the Carnegie Forum on Education and the Economy's Task Force on Teaching as a Profession released *A Nation Prepared: Teachers for the 21st Century* on May 16, 1986, which started standards-based accountability. Common Core State Standards are the latest result of the education reform that began with that critical publication in 1983.

In theory, test-based accountability is a way to ensure that schools are performing well while making it possible to reduce micromanagement, slash regulation, and boost school autonomy. In practice, any standardized assessment system is going to be constraining to some extent by requiring that schools teach certain skills or materials in the course of a given school year. Like it or not, the bottom line in K–12 education today is student achievement, and that achievement is being defined by standardized testing and the No Child Left Behind Act.

Common Core State Standards and the Librarian

It has become a necessity for school librarians to prove their worth and provide hard evidence about the role they fulfill within their school in implementing standards. School librarians play an essential role in ensuring that Common Core State Standards are integrated throughout all curriculum areas. Multiple literacies are addressed in the Common Core State Standards, which places school librarians in an optimum position to work with teachers to implement these standards. School librarians can assist with the integration of higher-order thinking skills into school curricula through information and technology literacy skills projects. For example, school librarians can work to ensure that library assignments are not "find and record," but rather that they are assignments that require students to locate information, analyze and process the information, and then synthesize a way to share the information with an audience as well as how to correctly apply the information to everyday situations. Research projects should be a learning experience where information and technology literacy skills are integrated into the curriculum in such a way that students are able to take part in the process of obtaining knowledge. Learning is a process, not a product, and school librarians are a critical component in this process. By collaborating with classroom teachers, school librarians are able to provide meaningful learning experiences that help prepare students to be successful in college and their careers.

Common Core State Standards in This Book

Each notation for the Common Core State Standard is abbreviated in this book. Each standard begins with the abbreviation CC to indicate it is a Common Core State Standard. Following the CC is the grade span for which the standard is intended. Next is the strand abbreviation as follows: Reading: Literature (R.L.); Reading: Informational Text (R.I.); Writing (W); Speaking and Listening (S.L.); Language (L); Writing for History, Social Studies, and Science/Technology (WH/SS/S/T); Reading for History, Social Studies, and Science/Technology (RH/SS/S/T). The last part is the standard number followed by the actual text of that standard.

For example, **CC.9–10.R.L.1** is:

CC = Common Core State Standard

9–10 = grade span

R.L. = Reading: Literature strand

1 = standard number

Note: All Common Core State Standards © 2010. National Governors Association Center for Best Practices and Council of Chief State School Officers. All rights reserved.

Information and Technology Literacy Standards

Some educators get so caught up in the technology aspect of a lesson that they forget to focus enough on academic rigor. Technology makes it easier to design meaningful projects and personalize the work for students, but the basis for the lesson needs to clearly address academic standards. A project should start with the Common Core State Standards and then incorporate technology tools that students will be able to use to learn the standards. Technology is called a tool because it should be used as a means of accomplishing a task. The use of technology should not be the task. There are technology literacy standards that should be incorporated into lesson plans in every curricular area, but unless you are teaching a technology class, they should not be the focus of the lesson. Several guidelines that could indicate technology should be integrated into the lesson include the following: technology should enhance the quality of learning in the classroom; technology should make lessons more enriching and engaging; technology should help students be more inquisitive, analytical, and creative; technology should allow students to collaborate, create, and apply their learning in real world contexts; and technology should allow you to collaborate and learn from others, share resources, and access the collective knowledge and resources available on the Internet.

International Society for Technology in Education National Education Technology Standards for Students

The lesson plans in this book list the International Society for Technology in Education (ISTE) National Education Technology Standards for Students (NETS-S) that are covered in that lesson. Each notation for the NETS-S is abbreviated in this book. Each standard begins with the abbreviation NETS to indicate it is an International Society for Technology in Education National Education Technology Standards for Students. There are six learning objectives of NETS–S: objective one is creativity and innovation; objective two is communication and collaboration; objective three is research and information fluency; objective four is critical thinking, problem solving, and decision making; objective five is digital citizenship; and objective six is technology operations and concepts. There are four standards (a through d) for each learning objective. The last part is the letter of the standard followed by the actual text of that standard. **NETS5.a** is:

NETS = International Society for Technology in Education National Education Technology Standards for Students

5 = learning objective number five: digital citizenship

a = standard letter

Note: All National Educational Technology Standards for Students, Second Edition © 2007. ISTE® (International Society for Technology in Education), www.iste.org. All rights reserved.

The Name Game

A certified professional who works in a school library setting is often known by many names: a librarian, a school librarian, a library specialist, a media specialist, a school library media specialist, an instructional technology specialist, a school library administrator, a library information specialist, a library curriculum specialist, a cybrarian, a teacher-librarian, and the list goes on. In fact, John McGinnis (2002) conducted a study that revealed that there were 93 unique titles by which school librarians were referring to themselves. In 2010, the American Association of School

Librarians (AASL) chose to officially adopt for the profession the title "school librarian." The organization's leadership made this decision after they conducted research that indicated confusion, misperceptions, and inconsistencies about various job titles in the school librarian profession. After carefully reviewing the data and identifying the advantages and disadvantages of various titles for the profession, the AASL Board of Directors chose this title to provide a common nomenclature and clear job description to other educators, administrators, and the public. The profession is currently transitioning from the term "school library media specialist," which has been our official designation going back to the first *Information Power* (1988). In order to avoid any confusion, throughout the book I will use the term "librarian" to refer to a professional filling the role of a leader, instructional partner, information specialist, teacher, and program administrator (as detailed in *Empowering Learners* 2009) in the school library.

1

What Are Networking Sites and Why Use Them?

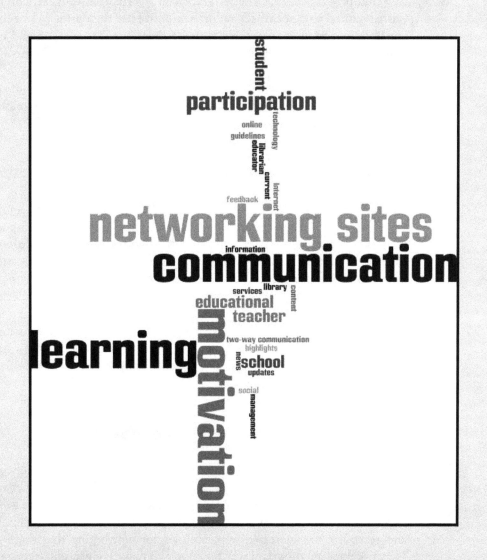

Networking is a global phenomenon and a mainstay of modern communication. The explosion of networking sites has changed the way we function on a daily basis. In 2010, Facebook hit a landmark when it signed up its 500 millionth member. Projections indicate the networking giant will eventually hit its next landmark of one billion users. Facebook is present in over 50 countries and is translated into over 100 languages around the world. And Facebook is just one of thousands of networking sites that people are using to communicate with their own personal community members. These statistics show that more patrons could be reached through the use of a networking site. From the growing number of subscribers to networking sites it seems this trend will continue, so if you want to reach your patrons you will need to use the resources they use. Everyone seems to be using networking media, so why not tap into these resources to achieve educational objectives? Networking sites can be used to keep in touch with members of your learning community, engage students, and enhance professional development for educators.

We are in the middle of a communication revolution as phone calls, emails, and even texts are becoming passé. Sending home newsletters and other forms of print communications are now considered wasteful and environmentally irresponsible. Lowered production costs, better and faster distribution of information, and less wasted natural resources make online options better than print. We need to design our library communication tools to make them current, relevant, and interesting. Nowadays it seems people want their entire community in on their conversations and their every activity, as many people post the most intimate details of their lives on their networking sites. Networking media permeate all aspects of our lives—affecting how we get information, how we learn, how we look for love and employment, how we shop, and how we socialize.

What Is Educational Networking?

Educational networking describes the use of social networking technologies and ideas for educational purposes. Educational networking sites are more secure sites that are often private (for viewing only by invited members) and are usually ad free. Social networking is a term used to describe websites that build online communities with the intent of building relationships among people with similar interests. These sites generally enable their subscribers: to post text, pictures, video, and various other forms of media content for others to view; to form and maintain relationships with other participants; and to engage in discussions around common interests with others. Some of the most popular social networks include the following: Myspace, Facebook, Twitter, Flickr, YouTube, Wikipedia, Blogster, LiveJournal, Foursquare, and Google Docs.

Networking Sites—Love Them or Hate Them

It seems there are two groups of people—those that love online networking and those that think there is nothing positive about it. People who love networking see the value of connecting with people across the world, appreciate the fact that they have a voice and can have it heard, see the opportunity to increase technology skills, and recognize the increased opportunities for networking that these sites offer. Networking is an important way for people to make connections outside their personal space—good for job searching, information gathering, obtaining homework assistance, making connections with people with similar interests and goals, and creating a great opportunity for self-expression. People against online networking sites think that people are no longer connecting in person, thus delaying or distorting the development of their social skills; claim that grammar and spelling are suffering due to the abbreviations being used (LOL, IMHO, msg, etc.); believe that people spend too much time inside on the computer instead of getting physical activity; recognize that dangerous predators exist online; and know cyberbullying often takes place on these sites. Chapter 2 will discuss some guidelines for Internet safety and help provide some justification for the incorporation of networking media into your school.

Benefits of Using Networking Sites in Education

We are no longer "just librarians" who can check out books to any students who walk through the library doors. We each have the power to reach our students (and students around the world) by using new technologies to enhance learning experiences, by using networking to get our voices and the voices of our students heard, and by using available online resources to open up a whole new world to our students. There are numerous benefits to incorporating networking technologies into the classroom to accomplish learning objectives, including but not limited to the following:

- **Knowledge and skills development**—Lesson plans incorporating networking sites can increase the depth of knowledge and level of understanding in content areas using the prescribed curriculum standards while also increasing technology skills. This book provides the Common Core State Standards as well as information and technology literacy standards met by each lesson plan to ensure students are building on their knowledge and skill level.

- **Motivation**—Networking sites entice students to complete the lesson by holding their interest. Engagement is often the prime justification for the integration of networking media into curriculum (see the following for the reasons motivation is so important). Students will spend more time on assignments that will be viewed by an authentic audience instead of just handing in an assignment to a teacher before throwing it in the trash once the grade is returned. Having such a large audience can push students to do their best to ensure they are proud of their work.

- **Connectivity**—Networking sites allow students to connect to other students and experts from around the world. Online networking sites allow students to connect to anyone with Internet access.

- **Familiarity**—Students are already familiar with many networking sites and want to show their current knowledge using these tools.

Terms to Know

Blog—A shortened form of the words *Web log*. A blog is a journal, diary, or other collection of writing and information that is usually displayed in reverse chronological order with the newest posts at the top. A typical blog combines text, images, links, and other media related to its topic.

Ebook—A shortened form of the words *electronic book*. An ebook is a book-length publication in digital form that is readable on computers or other electronic devices.

Educational networking—Term used to describe the use of social networking technologies and ideas for educational purposes.

Microblog—A short, concise journal, diary, or other collection of writing and information that is usually displayed in reverse chronological order with the newest posts at the top. The short exchange of information encourages more interaction between the blogger and followers.

Retweet—Sending out a tweet on Twitter that is the exact posting of someone else's tweet with their username attached to ensure they are given credit for the original tweet. A high rate of retweets can indicate a high success rate with getting information out using Twitter because the more times information is retweeted, the more people it reaches.

RSS feed—Stands for really simple syndication document. An RSS format is used to publish frequently updated information such as on a blog or other website.

Social networking—Term used to describe websites that build online communities with the intent of building relationships among people with similar interests.

Tweets—Term for posts on the social networking and microblogging site Twitter. Tweets are text-based posts of up to 140 characters displayed on a user's Twitter profile page.

Web 2.0—Term associated with Web applications sites that allow users to interact and collaborate with each other in a social online community.

Wiki—A website that is user friendly and easy to create. The word *wiki* is a Hawaiian word meaning quick.

Networking Sites to Know

Blogster (http://www.blogster.com) is a website that hosts an online community geared toward specific interest blogs. Blogster provides spam-free blogs and allows its users to create both profiles and blogs to build a more social environment. Users can add other users with the same interests as friends, chat with other users, join groups, upload photos on a gallery, and incorporate their blog RSS feed and Twitter and Flickr accounts.

Edmodo (http://www.edmodo.com) is a website that hosts a social learning community that has a similar interface to Facebook or Myspace. Users can create profiles and interact with others through the site. Students can submit assignments for teachers to grade and view grades. Teachers can post grades and assign homework to students.

Facebook (http://www.facebook.com) is one of the most popular social networking sites. Users can create a personal profile, add other users as friends, post status updates to share information with others, comment on friends' status updates, share pictures and videos, and exchange private messages with other users. Registered users must be at least 13 years old.

Flickr (http://www.flickr.com) is a website that allows users to upload, organize, share, and find images and videos. The site has over five billion images already uploaded. Users who sign up for a free account are allowed to upload 300 MB of images a month and two videos. Registered users must be at least 13 years old.

Foursquare (https://foursquare.com) is a popular location-based social networking website that uses a software application on mobile devices to allow users to "check in" at specific locations. Each check-in notifies friends of your location and provides suggestions for venues in the area. There are about 10 million registered users and nearly one billion recorded check-ins.

Google Docs (https://docs.google.com) is a website that hosts data storage for users to upload and collaborate on documents in real-time with other users. Documents up to 1 GB, such as text files, spreadsheets, presentations, drawings, or forms, can be uploaded to the site.

- **Cost effectiveness**—Networking sites are cost effective because most are free to anyone with Internet access. Using free networking sites allows cash-strapped districts to save money instead of purchasing expensive lesson plans and resources.

- **Convenience**—Networking sites are accessible through any Internet-accessible computer at any time, so learning can move beyond the school day.

- **Increased appropriate use**—When networking sites are used in schools, responsible and appropriate use of technology can no longer be assumed and must be taught directly to the students, thus increasing the appropriate use of technology. If we teach students how to use these technologies then they will be more responsible in their personal use.

- **Increased efficiency**—Students can have instant access to information when they need it. Students can access class information when they are absent or after school hours.

- **Increased self-expression**—Students love to have their voice heard, and the Internet opens their products to a worldwide audience. Networking sites allow connection to a large community as users with similar interests serve as an authentic audience.

- **Increased teamwork and cooperation**—Completing networking assignments in groups or corresponding with students in other places can increase teamwork and cooperation skills in students.

There are also numerous benefits to incorporating networking technologies into schools for communication, including but not limited to the following:

- **Increased pride**—Networking sites can instill pride in community through pictures, uplifting stories, and award recognitions.

- **Control**—Networking sites give schools control because instead of relying on what other media sources say, they can post their own information and respond to others.

- **Transparency**—Networking sites can offer transparency as parents and community members get a glimpse into what schools are doing on a daily basis. Networking sites can be used to promote positive aspects by highlighting library, school, and district successes.

- **Increased effectiveness of advocacy efforts**—Networking sites can reach a nearly limitless audience through people in your network forwarding digital information or passing on information through word-of-mouth to people who may not have networking access. Every time you use networking sites to engage someone online in a positive way, you have gained one more possible person in the fight for library funding should it ever face cuts.

Why Use Educational Networking in Your Classroom?

Any educator can tell you that the days of teachers standing in front of the room and lecturing for an hour while all the students enthusiastically take notes is long gone (as it probably should be). Today, educators have to incorporate project-based learning assignments and use students' interests to draw them into learning. Incorporating networking sites into lesson plans can increase students' motivation to learn by providing them an opportunity to learn using a technology they already love.

Love them or hate them, networking sites cannot be ignored. Today, 93 percent of teens use the Internet, and of those teens, 73 percent use networking sites (Lenhart et al. 2010). Teens use networking sites to not only interact with their peers but also to get information about issues that are important to them. Due to the popularity of networking sites with students, teachers may want to try to integrate networking sites into school-based learning just to see how engaged students will become when using a technology they love.

Why is motivation so important? Because keeping students in school may be one of the most urgent problems Americans currently face. Every nine seconds, one high school student drops out of school (Lehr et al. 2004). This is a shocking statistic that could be changed by simply incorporating resources and activities that students love. Our students live in a world where information is more social and more online. Like it or not, the fact remains that our students use these online networking sites and enjoy spending their free time on these sites. So why not use that passion to our advantage and incorporate those desires into an educational experience?

According to the White House (2010), 7,000 American students drop out of school *every day*. Recent research from "The Silent Epidemic: Perspective of High School Dropouts" (Bill and Melinda Gates Foundation 2006) indicated that 47 percent of dropouts stated their major reason for dropping out was that classes were not interesting, they were bored, and they felt disengaged from their classes, even though 88 percent of dropouts had passing grades. According to the same research, 69 percent of students say they are not motivated or inspired to learn in their classes. That means—as a result of low engagement, lack of motivation, and irrelevance of class work—over 6,000 capable young people will drop out of school *today*. Students just need to be introduced to the many new educational resources available that will make previously arduous topics interesting and exciting to them.

Individuals with fewer than 12 years of schooling have higher rates of unemployment and incarceration than individuals who receive a high school diploma. So why is student motivation such a good reason to incorporate technology? Because increased student motivation could increase the number of students who graduate and go on to be productive citizens in our communities. Online work also prepares students for college, where more professors expect students to finish assignments and take exams on the Internet. Classrooms that do not incorporate technology

Networking Sites to Know

LinkedIn (http://www.linkedin.com) is a social networking site that is primarily used for businesses and other professional organizations to connect to people needing their services or information about their services.

LiveJournal (http://www.livejournal.com) is a community publishing platform where users can keep a blog, journal, or diary and share their writing with other users.

Myspace, stylized My_____, (http://www.myspace.com) is one of the most popular social networking sites. Users can create a personal profile, add other users as friends, post pictures, and exchange messages. Registered users must be at least 13 years old.

Ning (http://www.ning.com) is an online platform for people to create their own social networks. Ning is no longer a free service, but there is a 30-day free trial and three different levels of paid accounts to choose from. Registered users must be at least 13 years old.

TweetDeck (http://www.tweetdeck.com) is a desktop application for managing user accounts on multiple social networks from one platform. TweetDeck allows you to read messages, organize messages, and cross-post new messages in Twitter, Facebook, Myspace, LinkedIn, Foursquare, and Google Buzz all in one location.

Twitter (http://twitter.com) is a social networking and microblogging service that enables its users to send and read messages up to 140 characters long (known as tweets).

Wikipedia (http://wikipedia.org) is a combination of the words *wiki* and *encyclopedia*. The site is a free online encyclopedia that allows contributors to collaboratively create the entries.

YouTube (http://www.youtube.com) is a free video-sharing website where users can upload, share, and view videos.

properly often have students who feel disconnected from the material. When students are able to get their hands on technology, they often are able to make the connection between what they are learning in class and what they already use or will be using in the real world. The students that we teach today grew up watching television, with its built-in commercial breaks and all its entertaining features. Students often shut down their brains if they are not engaged by the instructional delivery method. Educational networking assignments can increase student engagement and increase student access to academic information and curriculum resources. There is a price for not incorporating technology into the class, and it is the price students pay if they are not properly trained for college or for a job. If students are not educated enough to compete with other students for college spaces, scholarship allocations, and jobs, then we have failed them.

One of the frequent problems with new educational innovations is their expense, but you will not face a big funding challenge when adding educational networking sites into your classroom because most of them are *free*. Due to so many recent budget cuts, networking sites are a perfect alternative to purchasing expensive resources—networking sites are free, do not require processing, do not have to be inventoried, do not have to be replaced due to damage, cannot be stolen, are accessible anywhere and anytime, and contain not just one item to check out but a resource a whole class (or classes) can use at one time.

Be a Media Master

Effective communication is pivotal to a school these days. In today's climate it is important to circulate positive news about what is happening in the schools because so often people only hear the negative. A system should be set up to communicate with parents and other community members who may want to take advantage of library media center services but are not in the school on a daily basis. It takes less time to update networking sites and link to content than to contact local news stations and prepare a press release.

Networking sites offer unlimited communication possibilities. You need to inform your community members about what is happening in the library on a regular basis. Is there an excellent new resource available that you want your patrons to know about? Is there a great program you are offering after school? Networking media used for communication outreach can improve the consistency and quality of your communication. Having a strategic plan to incorporate networking media as a communication tool can relieve anxiety about how to promote your library program and events because you already have a communication system set up. Although it takes time and site promotion to build a community, once a community is established, time and effort to actually reach your community is minimal.

There are several steps for beginners to take when first setting up a networking site. Before beginning the process of creating a networking site for your library, you need to check your library and/or district policies. A word of warning: Do not skip these planning steps or it will cost you time and effort later.

1. **Choose your target audience.** Before you begin the process of setting up a networking site for communication purposes, you need to consider your target audience. Educators from K–12 through higher education need to communicate with students, staff, community stakeholders, and alumni. Public libraries will want to address the services that they offer their patrons—children's library services, special collection services, reference services, and so on.

2. **Learn about your target audience's needs.** You need to know your target audience so you know which sites are best to use and what content they need. We need to be where our patrons are, whether that is Twitter, Facebook, YouTube, or another site. Connecting with the connected means considering where 21st-century students spend their time and which environments they are open to learn in. To learn more about your target audience, you can form a focus group for input (you can bribe them with pizza or candy), do an online survey, and conduct informal interviews as patrons walk through the door. Through these formal and informal information-gathering sessions, you should try to discover information about your audience such as their experience level with networking sites, which sites they currently use, how they like to receive communications, and what information they need. You should also consider census data such as how many houses in the community have computers to determine if you will also need to continue to release information in print format.

3. **Choose the networking site that will most effectively reach your audience.** There are hundreds of sites to choose from, such as Myspace, Facebook, Twitter, LinkedIn, YouTube, Blogster, and more. Librarians need to make every effort to meet patrons in their comfort zones, even if it is new territory. You might have to investigate several sites to determine which will work best for your audience. The formal and informal data collection you did to learn about your audience's needs should narrow down the list quickly. You might need to try different sites and pilot some features to learn more about the sites. The best place to start to learn more about networking sites is to join the sites and learn from others. Even if you do not fully participate and just watch others (known as lurking and learning), you can get ideas for content to post and learn techniques for effective communication.

4. **Set content parameters.** You will need to set content areas for each of your target audience groups (students, parents, staff, stakeholders, alumni, etc.) to decide if you can address all the content on one site or if you need to set up different sites for each group in your audience. You need to decide—what does the library want its patrons to know? Information such as general facts (hours, policies), study tips, information about resources and how to access them, quick updates about changes in operating hours or services, information about upcoming programs and events, tutorials, guides, links for databases, reviews of new books, community events, articles on technology or books that may be of interest to patrons, ways people can donate and support the library, and so forth. Content should show that the library is a place that is current by releasing up-to-date, quality information consistently. You should also solicit content from patrons, not just push content out. See content suggestions that follow in this chapter.

5. **Set a responsibility plan for each contributor.** Networking sites can work if you are the sole employee or if you are one of a hundred employees in your facility. Although maintaining a networking site can be an overwhelming task if done alone, there are also many tools that make it more manageable (see management tips that follow). If your library has multiple employees, you should divide up the responsibilities to give everyone a voice. Although not every employee in a library needs to be involved in the networking site production, everyone that is involved needs to know their exact role. A set guideline will allow everyone to know what they are responsible for and how frequently to post. Students can also be contributors

by reviewing resources, interviewing staff members about what they are reading, and posting summaries of community events. You have to remember to do something to make it fun and keep people coming back.

6. **Set quality control guidelines for all contributors.** Providing guidelines and examples of good posts for contributors allows them to know exactly what to expect. Guidelines should be simple, such as the following: post should be less than 100 words, should be professional, should contain only appropriate language and grammar, should not contain any information that could be harmful to others, and so forth. The overall guideline for contributors should be that they should be proud of their digital footprint, so ask them to read their post and ask themselves "Am I proud to say I wrote this post?" If they cannot answer yes to that question then they should not post it. The guidelines should make sure the contributors keep it professional but do not restrict them so much that they feel they cannot make it fun. If posts are too formal they will seem stuffy, cold, and all business. Instead of guidelines, another option is to moderate submissions so that one person is reading all comments before they are actually posted to ensure that there are no biases, comments with inappropriate language, misinformation, and so on.

7. **Create your site.** Build it and they will come—you must post your site in order to begin to build an audience. Be honest about your time/abilities. Do not try to set everything up at once, and do not feel bad about not being on every networking site out there. Do not try to do everything at once. There are hundreds of sites to choose from, so you need to know how to get started on the sites and also be able to show your patrons how to follow your sites. I created handouts for setting up accounts on the sites used in this book to get you started, and these handouts can be edited to give to your patrons. The handouts can be found in the appendix as well as on my blog at http://networkedlibrary.wordpress.com.

8. **Promote your site to build a community.** The main point of networking sites is to create a community. A network is no good without people in it. Every site you start will go through growing pains where you have to work hard to build a network of people. Even Facebook did not grow to 500 million users overnight. Facebook started as a small site intended for students at Harvard and through word-of-mouth grew exponentially. You have to work to get the word about your site out there to build your followers. Put links to your site everywhere you can—websites, newsletters, email, and listservs—as well as verbally reminding patrons to check out the sites. Go to Parent Teacher Student Association meetings and host a technology night to show community members how to sign up and use the sites. Give it time because it does not happen overnight, but do not beat a dead horse. If you create a site and give it an allotted period of time to build a community but it just is not well received, then move on to a new site or totally redesign your approach with that current site. Do not waste your time on sites that just do not work for you.

9. **Set your goals and standards to measure for success.** You will need to periodically assess your success using networking media as a communication tool in order to revise and improve the services you offer. You will need to have a plan to outline how you will measure success. Keep up a cycle of assessment by reviewing data gathered through formal assessment tools such

as online surveys, focus groups, and analysis tools. Continuously conduct informal assessment by asking random patrons if they have noticed the networking sites and what they do and do not like about the communications that they have seen. Set a standard/goal for how many posts you want in a specific time period (one per day is a good starting place). Frequent posting provides consistency and keeps readers coming back often. Set guidelines for posts (keep it professional, keep it unbiased, keep it short, keep it fun, inappropriate posts will result in loss of the privilege to post, etc.). Set other target goals such as number of followers, number of questions/comments by patrons, number of times information is shared (search the Internet to see if your information is getting reposted, linked to, and retweeted), and number of people attending events and programs that you promoted on your networking sites. Accessing these numbers gives a picture of how the media is being received. Google analytic (http://www.google.com/analytics) and Facebook analytics measure traffic on sites, and Twitter will have one soon. You can embed these analytics onto your sites. Analytics provides evidence to justify your efforts.

10. **Engage your audience.** You want to attract people to your site and keep them as regular readers. Of course, you want to analyze your audience to determine the content they need and want. Readers may not be interested in everything you post about, so put fun information on your site to keep readers engaged. Create communities that involve your users and you will learn more about your patrons and their needs through the two-way communication. Creating sites that allow two-way communication shows your patrons that you value their opinion. There are patrons who may not choose to visit the library to complete a paper suggestion form or speak with you face-to-face but feel comfortable doing so online anonymously. Allowing patrons to comment on services allows you to improve the services your program offers. A good motto to have is "there is no best, only better." Every media program can be improved upon, but evaluation is needed to identify areas for improvement. Use the results to better your library program, and make sure you share a summary of the results and changes that were made due to the survey your patrons filled out.

11. **Keep your site current and continuously promote it.** Stick to the standard you set for the number of posts each day or week to ensure that your content is current and frequent enough to keep your audience informed. If you work in a school with a summer break, it is fine to slow the frequency over the break, but do not stop all together or you will lose readers that may not re-subscribe when school starts back up. Posts do not have to post right away. You can draft and post later by setting a posting schedule. See the following management suggestions. Reposting important information is also a good idea for the summers. Make sure your site does not look neglected by taking the time to read and respond frequently to any comments or questions. A network is no good without people in it. You must promote your YouTube channel, your Twitter account, your Facebook page, your website, your blog, and so on. Other ways to promote your networking sites include going to Parent Teacher Student Association meetings, hosting a technology night, printing a letter to go home with students, and putting links on all your other webpages (for example, on your blog put links to YouTube, Facebook, and so on, and then on Facebook put the links to all the other sites again).

Suggestions for Content to Post

Probably the most difficult part of setting up a networking site is trying to determine what to post. There are several kinds of information that need to be included in a networking site: information that is needed by all your patrons (hours of operation and policies), information that is fun and entertaining (contests and patron spotlights), information that should be available on an as-needed basis (pathfinders and resource instructions), and some information that is helpful to you (feedback and surveys). But remember, networking tools are really about a two-way conversation, not just information distribution. Many librarians put off creating a networking site for their library because they are afraid that they will not have enough content to post. The following is a list of suggestions for content to post:

- **General library news.** General information includes standards and changes in library hours, policies, and services. Also post about events and programs produced by the library or taking place inside the library.

- **Updates that offer transparency.** Give updates on learning that is taking place in the school and library as well as student and staff accomplishments. For example, many classrooms have Facebook pages and give status reports on what is happening in the classroom so parents can keep up with the learning that is taking place throughout the day.

- **Feedback.** Post a survey or questions to ask your patrons how you can better serve them through your library media program. There are patrons who may not choose to visit the library to complete a paper suggestion form or speak with you face-to-face but feel comfortable doing so anonymously online. Allowing patrons to comment on services allows you to improve the services your program offers.

- **Highlight resources and services.** Post a weekly "Wednesday's Website," a "Tuesday Technology Tip," and/or a "Friday Fun Fact" that includes an interesting fact and which resource in the library media center that fact was found in (used to highlight different resources available for checkout). Networking sites can be used to reach potential new users, so resources should be highlighted in order to get them to come to the physical facility. Show your patrons that the library has changed from the stereotypical warehouse of old books to a 21st-century learning center of the school by keeping a well-weeded collection offering some of the latest resources. You would be surprised how adding audiobooks, ebooks, popular magazines, online databases, and graphic novels to your collection will really draw in some of the dormant readers in your school. Your networking sites should include links to online library resources (such as databases) and helpful links to other research tools available for free on the Web.

- **Media staff updates.** Show your friendly and helpful attitude with personal "Behind the Scenes" updates such as "Just finished processing 45 new books for the career section. Come in and check them out." or "Attended a webinar on using Glogster. Come in and let me share some great tips with you." This section of your site could have a catchy name like "Stories from the Stacks."

- **Book discussions.** Set up a blog area for students at your school to comment on books that they have read. Post a question like "What are you reading right now?" "What is your favorite book of all time?" "If you could be any character from a book who would it be?" and "What is your favorite opening line of a book?" to increase interaction between fans. Of course, not every reader is going to love every book. With a whole library full of good books, you may want to try to avoid posting really negative reviews of books. If a patron is writing a review and they do not like the book, ask them to keep the tone positive and include a statement such as "While I would not recommend this particular title, there are a couple other similar books you might want to check out such as ..."

- **Book promotions.** Post a blog series, called something catchy like "Reading Raves" or "Rad Reads," that highlights what students, faculty, and staff like to read for fun. Make your book talks accessible to a large audience and make them more interesting to technology-savvy students by creating podcasts of the book talks. The books with book talks will probably stay in constant circulation as patrons get "hooked" by the podcasts and cannot wait to read the whole book themselves. Students would love to post book talks, publish reviews of new resources, conduct interviews with staff, and so on, and these activities give them ownership. If you post student work, interviews, and other content that involves your patrons then they have a vested interest and will tell their friends, who will tell their friends, and so on.

- **Patron highlights.** Have a "Patron Spotlight" that features patrons, their picture, and some information about what they are currently reading or their favorite books. These types of sections allow patrons to have ownership of the site and encourage patrons to visit the physical facility to meet featured patrons or become a featured patron themselves. An "Overheard at the Library" section with recent patron quotes can share some personal patron stories, such as a student with a new sibling at home who was heard saying, "The library is my escape because it is the only place I can go to study without a baby crying in the background."

- **A virtual tour.** Create a virtual tour of your library media center to use as an introduction during orientation and to show to any new students entering the school. Post this tour on your library media center website, blog/wiki, YouTube, or similar site so anyone not able to physically visit your school can at least get a virtual tour of your program. A very simple tour can be created using PowerPoint using still pictures with written descriptions. More elaborate tours can be created using MovieMaker or other video-creation software and recorded narration.

- **Encourage support.** Networking sites are a great way to recruit volunteers and encourage support. Post requests for volunteers and items that you need, as well as government officials who need to be contacted in order to keep funding for libraries. Make sure to thank contributors and volunteers on your networking sites also.

Advice for Management

- Each district and/or school should set up specific policies that support the effective use of networking sites in schools. The first step for many schools is to unblock useful sites, such as Twitter and YouTube, that can be utilized for communication, teaching, and learning. The next step would be to make sure your acceptable use policy includes networking technologies (see chapter 2 for an example).

- Using a management program to participate in multiple networking spaces from one place will increase your effectiveness and decrease your time and effort. Using a service like TweetDeck (http://www.tweetdeck.com) can help you read, write, and organize messages posted online in Twitter, Facebook, Myspace, LinkedIn, Foursquare, and Google Buzz all at once. TweetDeck allows you to cross-post messages in more than one place all at once. However, it is best to have some unique content on each site (Facebook, Twitter, etc.) in case people follow all sites. RSS feeds can also help with management by syndicating content automatically as well as by tracking the number of subscribers who receive the feed.

2

Guidelines to Keep Your Students and Yourself Safe When Integrating Networking Sites in the Classroom

The Internet is a scary place for some teachers, parents, and even students. We cannot allow fear to dictate our progress, nor can we hang onto our current practices and just hope the waves of changes do not drown us. Our profession involves teaching students to use the tools of the real world. It is unimaginable that a teacher or parent would turn a child loose using a stove, a table saw, or even scissors without some instruction on how to use the tool and supervision until it is mastered. Parents and teachers should feel the same way about the Internet. It is a tool that requires training and supervision to master. Librarians need to be leading the pack when it comes to teaching students to use technology tools and preparing our students for the 21st century.

As you have already read in this book, there are numerous benefits to incorporating networking sites into classrooms, but there are also some risks that need to be addressed. Part of the burden of being responsible is that one must always balance potential advantages and risks. The Internet is a tool that allows children to connect with, communicate with, and create with others around the world who share their passions, interests, and talents while at the same time potentially opening lines of communication with strangers who may want to inflict harm on them. If we do not teach students about appropriate use, they will surely encounter exactly that which we are most scared of and not know how to deal with the situation. Everyone should be concerned with cyber safety, but many children do not truly understand the dangers that exist online. As librarians, we need to be the leaders in providing instruction to our students in the effective, efficient, and ethical use of technology resources. Educators need to teach proper and purposeful techniques for using social networking in schools or students might learn improper usage somewhere else.

Of course, the Internet offers inappropriate content students can see as well as a free forum for students to write inappropriate content, but they can hear inappropriate conversations on the street corner and write anything they want with a pen and paper. This chapter is not meant to address every issue that will be encountered online but is meant to provide a basis for including networking sites in lesson plans. There are entire books available on cyber safety and responsible Internet behavior that provide more information on the subject. I am not going to cover every rule but rather provide some of the reasoning behind incorporating these technologies in your school and for setting guidelines for safety.

What Are the Issues with Using Networking Sites?

Many online communities post material that is not appropriate for children or that many parents would find objectionable. This can include obscene language, racist or violent text or images, and a wide range of sexual content including pornography. Of course, every social networking site is not appropriate for classroom use, but the same can be said for books—not every book is appropriate for classroom use. So should educators block all books from the classroom? As ridiculous as that sounds, that is exactly what is happening with counties that block all websites that are classified as any form of a networking site. This means they are blocking a lot of learning opportunities because of the label "social networking." What should happen is that educators should have the ability to select appropriate websites and incorporate them into the educational process, just like they do with books and other resources. While it is not educationally relevant for schools to allow students to update their online profiles while in school, schools are disallowing the very technology that students are using for their informal communications and learning instead of harnessing that interest into an educational experience. Several issues that will be discussed include fear of cyberspace, cyberbullying, the consequences associated with creating a negative digital footprint through the use of networking sites, the use of the Internet to plagiarize assignments, laws that might inhibit educators from using networking sites in their classroom, and school and county policies that might restrict the use of networking sites in classrooms.

Fear of Cyberspace

It is fear that guides many of the decisions about educational technology: fear that we will be left behind globally by countries more committed to technology integration and also fear that our students will somehow be scarred by its use. Every day you can turn on your television and see all the dangers children face when on the Internet. Television shows, like NBC's *To Catch a Predator,* feed the fears of parents everywhere of having their child exposed to a predator. It is a real fear and certainly a serious danger that we have to prepare our children to encounter. The facts, however, support evidence that over 90 percent of child predators are family members or close family friends, rather than strangers met online (Child Molestation Research and Prevention Institute 2011). The best way to defend our children against predators is to educate them by teaching them of the dangers and how to avoid dangerous situations. We cannot lock children in a tower away from all the dangers of the outside world, so we must teach them to be responsible individuals. Everyone must understand their responsibilities for conducting themselves online in order to be good digital citizens. We have to face our fears head on if we are going to be a part of the 21st century.

Bullying in Cyberspace

A significant issue of increasing concern is cyberbullying. Bullies are no longer confined to confronting their victims in school yards or hallways when no adults are watching. Through the Internet, they now have an open forum to threaten, harass, and stalk their victims. The ability to post to blogs, websites, and social media sites anonymously or through a made-up identity often creates situations that can encourage bad behavior by eliminating consequences for taking responsibility for one's actions and written words. The anonymity features of many social networking sites allow users to insult and harass people in ways they might not in person. The effects of cyberbullying can be far reaching and long lasting. In recent news, the mother of a Canadian teenager said taunts on a popular social networking site, including at least one that suggested the girl kill herself, contributed to her 15-year-old daughter's suicide.

A Digital Footprint

Never before in history have kids had the ability to create and publish so much content, so easily. The high usage of social networking sites and the posting of so much seemingly harmless information on these sites has created dangerous situations for many trusting users. Children can make unwise decisions about what

---

Terms to Know

Creative Commons—Licensed content such as videos, images, and music that are made available to the public for free legal sharing, reuse, and remixing.

Cyberbullying—Posting comments or pictures online that are harassing, intimidating, insulting, defaming, embarrassing, or hurtful to another person.

Cyberspace—Used to describe the virtual environments found online.

Digital citizenship—A standard of appropriate behavior when using technology.

Digital footprint—Trail of information about yourself left online for others to see. Digital footprints include emails and attachments, uploaded videos and images, profiles created, forum posts, and so on. Students need to learn what a digital footprint is so they know how they create a respectable digital footprint of which they are proud.

they post online (often when encouraged by their peers). This includes posting pictures of themselves or friends in racy or incriminating situations; publishing too much information about themselves, which opens the door for predators to use that information to locate them; bragging about real or made-up improper actions; and making threatening or harassing remarks to or about someone. All of these situations could have very negative and damaging consequences. Students are being turned down by employers for jobs, internships, and even interviews because of the information employers are finding about students on their social networking accounts.

A digital footprint is a trail of information about yourself left online for others to see. Digital footprints include emails and attachments, uploaded videos and images, profiles created, forum posts, and so on. Students need to learn what a digital footprint is so they know how to create a respectable digital footprint of which they are proud. Students should be encouraged to create a positive self-image by letting viewers see their best qualities, not their worst. A positive digital footprint will show that students care about their reputation and what their peers, family members, teachers, and future employers think about them. A good rule to follow is this: if it is not something you would want your grandmother to see or read, do not post it.

Students should search themselves by Googling (http://www.google.com) their "full name" (in quotation marks so it does not get split up) + their city and state to see what shows up. Also have students search themselves using a people search engine such as one of these:

123People (http://www.123people.com/)

Pipl (http://pipl.com)

Spokeo (http://www.spokeo.com/)

Conducting these searches can help students assess and clean up a negative digital footprint or celebrate a positive digital footprint.

Plagiarism, Copyright Laws, Fair Use, and Creative Commons

A common fear of educators using Internet resources is that students will plagiarize information by simply cutting and pasting information verbatim. Educators should be teaching students about copyright laws, fair use guidelines, Creative Commons, intellectual property, and citing sources. Educators should also design projects that involve creating new products and information, not just regurgitating facts. We need to get away from cut-and-paste activities that encourage plagiarism and into something that students create and *enjoy* creating, such as through the integration of networking sites into the classroom.

Copyright laws protect the authors or creators of an original work by granting them the right to determine if and how their work is copied, distributed, or adapted. For full details on copyright laws see the United States Copyright Office website (http://www.copyright.gov). Anyone wishing to use copyrighted materials must first get permission from the author/creator.

Fair use guidelines offer educators and students some flexibility in regards to the copyright laws. For full details on the fair use guidelines see the United States Copyright Office website (http://www.copyright.gov/fls/fl102.html). Fair use allows educators to use some copyrighted materials for educational purposes, without asking permission. Fair use also allows students to use some copyrighted material to create new materials that add value to or repurpose the original work, without asking for permission. It is often hard to determine if copyrighted materials fall under the fair use guideline, but this document, *Tool for Reasoning Fair Use* (http://copyrightconfusion.wikispaces.com/file/view/Tool+for+reasoning+Fair+Use.pdf), can help with that determination.

One alternative to dealing with strict copyright laws and fair use guidelines, which are hard to interpret, is to use Creative Commons licensed materials. Creative Commons includes licensed content such as videos, images, and music that are made available to the public for free legal sharing, reuse, and remixing. The use of Creative Commons content demonstrates respect for intellectual property while also recognizing the need to share and build upon current knowledge. Librarians should be teaching about Creative Commons licenses and helping teachers and students access the major portals with Creative Commons content. Creative Commons (http://search.creativecommons.org) is a website that offers a convenient way to search one website to access Creative Commons licensed images, videos, and other media that can be found on Wikimedia Commons, Flickr, Google Web, Google Images, Blip.tv, Jamendo, and Spinxpree websites.

Librarians need to ensure that students understand that there are different licenses that can be obtained through Creative Commons and that each license provides different restrictions for the use of that licensed material. Students should be shown the Creative Commons website (http://creativecommons.org) and shown each of the license icons for easy recognition. There are six main Creative Commons licenses; here is a general overview of all six in order from least restrictive to most restrictive:

1. **Attribution** is the least restrictive of the licenses because it allows others to distribute, display, perform, remix, tweak, and use any derivative works based upon it, even commercially, as long as they credit you for the original creation.

2. **Attribution-ShareAlike** is a license that allows others to distribute, display, perform, remix, tweak, and use any derivative works based upon it, even commercially, as long as they credit you for the original creation *and* license their new creations under the identical terms (thus any derivatives will also allow commercial use).

3. **Attribution-NoDerivs** is a license that allows others to download, copy, display, and distribute your works, commercial and noncommercial, as long as they give credit to you and they do not change the works in any way.

4. **Attribution-NonCommercial** is a license that allows others to distribute, display, perform, remix, tweak, and use any derivative works based upon it, *except* commercially, as long as they credit you for the original creation.

5. **Attribution-NonCommercial-ShareAlike** is a license that allows others to distribute, display, perform, remix, tweak, and use any derivative works based upon it, *except* commercially, as long as they credit you for the original creation *and* license their new creations under the identical terms (thus any derivatives will also prohibit commercial use).

6. **Attribution-NonCommercial-NoDerivs** is the most restrictive of licenses, only allowing others to download, copy, display, and distribute your works as long as they give credit to you and they do not change the works in any way or use them commercially.

Whether claiming fair use or using Creative Commons content, attribution of all works used is required. Citing sources builds academic integrity and demonstrates respect for the intellectual property of others. There are several free citation generators that may help with citing sources:

- Son of Citation Maker (http://citationmachine.net) is an interactive tool that allows the user to create proper citations in MLA (Modern Language Association), APA (American Psychological Association), Chicago, and Turabian formats by filling in blanks with the required information.

- Bibme (http://www.bibme.org) is a fully automatic bibliography generator and citation maker that anticipates sources as you type. The site can be used for MLA, APA, Chicago, and Turabian formats.

- EasyBib (http://easybib.com) is a fully automatic bibliography generator and citation maker that anticipates sources as you type. The site can be used for MLA, APA, and Chicago/Turabian formats.

What Do the Laws Require Teachers to Do?

Many teachers are under the false impression that districts are required by law to block the majority of the Internet. Many responsible adults are under the impression that if they allow students to access the Internet in class, post student work to the Internet, or assign work that requires access to social networking tools, then they are breaking one of the many laws put into place to help protect children. But this is not correct. Here is a brief overview of the three laws that apply to minors using online resources:

The Children's Internet Protection Act (CIPA) is a federal law that addresses minors' access to offensive content over the Internet on school and library computers. It applies only to minors in schools and libraries that apply for e-rate funds (the e-rate fund program provides discounts to assist schools and libraries in the United States to obtain affordable telecommunications and Internet access). The law requires an Internet safety policy that addresses the following: blocking or filtering Internet access to pictures and information that are obscene, child pornography, or harmful to minors; a method for monitoring online activities; and a security system that restricts unauthorized access to hacking and unauthorized use of personal information. These policies should apply for all computers that are accessed by minors. Find the full text of the law at the Internet Free Expression Alliance (2001) website at http://ifea.net/cipa.pdf

The Children's Online Privacy Protection Act of 1998 (COPPA) is a federal law that restricts the online collection of personal information from children under 13 years of age. The law allows children under 13 to legally give out personal information but only with their parents' permission. To avoid a large mass of paperwork, many websites, such as YouTube and Facebook, require users to be over the age of 13 in order to obtain an account. Find the full text of the law at the Federal Trade Commission (2011) website at http://www.ftc.gov/ogc/coppa1.htm.

The Family Educational Rights and Privacy Act (FERPA) is a federal law that protects the privacy of student education records. It applies to all schools that receive funds under an applicable program of the U.S. Department of Education. The act addresses children's education records, providing parents and students the right to inspect, review, question, and have updated incorrect records. It also states that schools must receive permission from a parent or guardian to release information from a student's education record. Find the full text of the law at the Electronic Privacy Information Center (2011) website at http://epic.org/privacy/education/ferpa.html.

CIPA, COPPA, and FERPA were created to protect children, not restrict their learning experiences. These acts do not state that teachers cannot publish student's names, videos, work, pictures, and so forth online. These acts do not prohibit schools from using Twitter, YouTube, email, or any other networking sites that are often blocked by school Internet filters. If all networking sites were harmful to minors, would President Obama (http://www.facebook.com/barackobama) have a Facebook Fan page, or would the Library of Congress have a YouTube channel (http://www.youtube.com/user/LibraryOfCongress?blend = 1&ob = 5)?

These laws do require schools to do the following:

- Have a filter system in place to block pornography and other obscene images from minors (this applies only to schools receiving federal e-rate funds)

- Ensure there is an acceptable use policy in place

- Notify parents that their child's work, likeness, and name will be shared throughout the year, and let them know the procedure for opting out (schools should have the permission release provided and signed as part of the student registration packet)

- Have a security system in place to protect private information

- Have a monitoring system in place to ensure that the Internet is being used appropriately

Fight the Filter

Administrators are already overburdened with daily discipline, parent concerns, and other administrative tasks, so utilizing Internet filters that block the majority of Internet resources provides the easiest means for ensuring that no students are accessing inappropriate information. Many schools have such strict access to Internet resources that patrons are blocked even from many purely educational sites. Restrictions do need to be in place to protect students from online predators, pornographic materials, and other inappropriate and harmful content, but access needs to be carefully analyzed to allow access to sites that meet the educational needs of patrons. There is valuable information on the Internet that will help students learn and encourage them to learn on their own.

Librarians are known to lead the fight against censorship of books, and blocking learning opportunities through the use of Internet filters can be considered another form of censorship. The burden of convincing administrators to decrease the parameters of the school's Internet filter to allow access to more educational resources often falls to the school librarian and top technology-savvy teachers in the school. Administrators need to see examples of learning opportunities using networking sites if they are to become the supporters needed to allow access to these sites at school. The lesson plans in this book provide those examples needed to show administrators how Common Core State Standards can be taught through the integration of networking sites.

Policies

Educators should make sure students sign an acceptable use policy and understand the consequences for not adhering to the set policies. You are never going to have a policy that covers everything, but cover the basics that are built around the premise of being responsible for all actions at all times. School officials understand that students may find ways to go through Internet filters and firewalls. But if students do so, they do it knowing that they are going against school policies and safeguards and thus will receive consequences for their actions. Schools should have a discipline system in place to restrict students found to be using the Internet inappropriately. Students need to understand what appropriate use is and what the consequences are for inappropriate behaviors. Table 2.1 is an example of an acceptable use policy for students.

Policies and guidelines should be looked at and adapted each year to address new and emerging technologies. Acceptable use policies usually do not take networking sites into consideration, so it is a necessity to either update the policy or create a separate contact to deal with networking site issues. Younger children may not have the skills required to avoid inappropriate sites and situations, so Internet filtering is more important for elementary-aged students. As students mature and gain more knowledge and experience to judge appropriate ways to use the Internet, they need more freedom to show their responsibility. All students need guidance to become responsible digital citizens, and they must also buy into the fact that use of the Internet at school is a privilege, not a right. One way to make sure students

---

TABLE 2.1 Example of an Acceptable Use Policy for Students Using Computers at School

I, _____, accept and agree to abide by the following rules:

I realize that the use of computers at school is a privilege, not a right. My privilege to access my computer account is directly linked to my responsibility using that account. I accept that inappropriate behavior may lead to penalties, including suspension of access to my computer account, disciplinary action, and/or legal action. I understand that all computer activity is monitored.

I understand that the following offenses will result in disciplinary actions:

Offense: Violating any federal, state, or local statutes.

Offense: Searching for inappropriate information or images, including searching for or accessing offensive, harassing, profane, pornographic, obscene, or disparaging material.

Offense: Posting inappropriate information or images, including using profane, abusive, threatening, harassing, pornographic, obscene, or impolite material.

Offense: Using someone else's log-on information or sharing your log-on information with someone else.

Offense: Damaging computer equipment, files, data, or the network in any way, including intentionally accessing or transmitting computer viruses or other harmful files or programs.

Offense: Attempting to access information protected by privacy laws.

Offense: Violating copyright or the intellectual property of another individual or organization without permission.

All offenses will be referred to an administrator to determine disciplinary actions.

I release the school and the school system and all other organizations and individuals from any liability or damages that may result from using computers on campus. In addition, I will accept full responsibility and liability for the results of my actions with regard to the use of my computer account.

Student Signature _____ Date _____

I, _____ as the legal guardian of the above student, understand that my student will have access to a computer account during the school day to meet educational objectives and that the student has agreed to the acceptable use policy as outlined above.

Guardian Signature _____ Date _____

---

know what online behavior is expected of them and get them to agree to this behavior is to have them sign a responsible use contract. Table 2.2 is an example of a contract for students to sign agreeing specifically to use networking sites (obviously it can be adapted to apply to the Internet in general or other specific aspects of the Internet) responsibly while at school.

Most students appreciate the privilege of using computers and networking sites and the respect afforded to them in doing so. Most students protect this privilege by ensuring they do not abuse their rights to use networking sites appropriately, but these signed contracts ensure that they understand what appropriate use is.

We need to empower students to function responsibly in a world where they have to make many decisions for themselves on a daily basis. The world is full of choices, and we cannot be there to guide children through every decision that they have to make. We must teach children to use the Internet responsibly so when they are not in school or when their formal schooling is complete, they will have the skills needed to be responsible digital citizens in their personal lives.

Guidelines for Student Use of Networking Sites

Many social networking sites are blocked in schools, but where there is a will there is a way. If students want to access these sites, they will find a place to do it, whether it is at home, on their cell phone, at the public library, or at a friend's house. We

---

TABLE 2.2 Example of a Responsible Use Contract for Students Using Networking Sites at School

I, _____, accept and agree to abide by the following rules:

I realize that the use of networking sites at school is a privilege, not a right. My privilege to access networking sites is directly linked to my responsibility using those sites. I understand that social networking sites may be used in the classroom only with approval and supervision of the regular classroom teacher. Use of networking sites during the school day should only be used for school assignments and not for personal use (meaning for any reason not relating to my school work). I accept that inappropriate behavior may lead to penalties, including suspension of access to the Internet or my computer account, disciplinary action, and/or legal action. I understand that all computer activity is monitored.

I understand that the following offenses will result in disciplinary actions:

Offense: Using networking sites for personal use (meaning for any reason not relating to my school work).

Disciplinary Actions: Students who abuse their privilege to access networking sites by using them for personal means at school will receive a written discipline referral for the first offense. A second offense will result in Internet access being disabled. The length of time for the suspension of Internet access is based on administrative discretion. Students who attempt to bypass the Internet filter will have their access to their computer account disabled. The length of time for the suspension of computer access is based on administrative discretion.

All other offenses will be referred to an administrator to determine disciplinary actions.

Offense: Using networking sites to search for inappropriate information or images, including searching for or accessing offensive, harassing, profane, pornographic, obscene, or disparaging material.

Offense: Using networking sites to post inappropriate information or images, including using profane, abusive, threatening, harassing, pornographic, obscene, or impolite material.

I release the school and the school system and all other organizations and individuals from any liability or damages that may result from using networking sites on campus. In addition, I will accept full responsibility and liability for the results of my actions with regard to the use of networking sites.

Student Signature _____ Date _____

I, _____ as the legal guardian of the above student, understand that networking sites will be used during the school day to meet educational objectives and that the student has agreed to the responsible use contract as outlined above.

Guardian Signature _____ Date _____

---

need to support students' desires to use these sites for educational learning opportunities. We need to empower students to keep themselves safe through guidance of the dangers that are present and how to avoid them. We need to stop dictating what resources they can and cannot access for learning and start guiding, supporting, and empowering students to follow safety guidelines while online. Students are going to use social networking sites or be exposed to mature content at some point, so we need to educate them to make responsible choices. Rather than assuming that schools will be able to deny access and participation in any form of online socializing for the first 18 years of a child's life, educators should be having open, calm dialogues that lay out some simple guidelines for students to participate in an online community. Following some simple precautions can make social networking a safe and enriching experience. Most online rules are commonsense rules that should be applied in and out of cyberspace. The following general guidelines should be implemented by educators who want to ensure the safety of their students:

- All educators should preview all sites or resources before children access them.

- All educators should monitor children's online usage and profile pages.

- Educators need to have a clear reason for implementing online resources to meet specific learning objectives and explain those reasons to the students.

Enforcing these guidelines may not be popular with students, so it is important to explain that safety is your key concern—both physically and in cyberspace. Schools serve as in loco parentis when the students enter the door, so we must ensure they are properly monitored on the Internet as well as in the physical classroom. Just like you would not take your students on a field trip to a new place and let them go off by themselves, you should not turn students loose on the Internet without guidance and supervision.

General Guidelines to Follow When Online

When working with students, we want to empower them to independently use online tools not only at school, but also in life. Here is a quick list of key discussion points that should take place in your classroom before students begin online assignments that might expose them to new situations such as networking communities:

- Review best practices in posting information online (see the following guidelines for discussion points).

- Teach students to be their own filtering tool by teaching students to hit Ctrl + W to close the window and continue if something inappropriate does pop up.

- Discuss what cyberbullying is and encourage students to report bullying to an adult.

Adults should provide guidelines for children to follow when online so that they know exactly what behavior is expected of them. Every teacher knows that they should provide a short list (less than five) of rules that students are expected to know by heart and adhere to each and every day. Guidelines include the following:

1. **The first basic rule is do not do something in cyberspace that you would consider wrong or illegal in everyday life.** This rule includes these standards: do not use rude or offensive language, call people names, lie about

them, send embarrassing pictures of them, or do anything else to try to hurt them. Ask students to consider how the information that is posted online might be interpreted by others, including teachers, friends, family members, potential employers, and college administrators. Student need to understand that a digital footprint lasts forever, so they need to think before they post pictures of underage drinking or other illegal or inappropriate activity.

2. **Treat every individual just like a stranger you would meet in person.** Be aware that people may not be who they say they are. Do not allow yourself to stay in a situation where you feel uncomfortable; if you are uneasy about a situation, tell an adult.

3. **Adhere to copyright restrictions.** This includes these standards: do not copy information from the Internet and claim it as yours, and always follow copyright laws when downloading material, including software, games, movies, or music, from the Internet.

4. **Make sure your online profiles and usernames follow safety guidelines.** Do not post your full name, birthday, personal information that reveals your identity, or location in your profile or username. Even seemingly innocent email addresses might tell someone else your real name, where you go to school or work, or where you live.

As educators, we are professionals who serve as role models to hundreds of students each year and thousands of students over the course of our careers. Thus, we have a professional image to uphold and must consider that image every time we are online. The same rules apply to you as they do to students. Do not say anything that you would not say in a public place such as your classroom. Keep all posts professional and never criticize students, co-workers, or school policies. Many educators have a false sense of security because they think privacy settings will keep their information from ever being seen by the masses. Educators need to understand that some information that they assume is private can actually be viewed by students or their parents. Before you post something online, you should imagine your students, their parents, your co-workers, your administrators, or a school board member reading that post.

Additional Resources Worth Checking Out
3DWiredSafety: http://www.3dwriting.com/wiredsafety/blog
10 Interesting Ways and Tips to Teach Internet Safety in the Classroom: https://docs.google.com/present/view?id=0AcIS3lrIFkCIZGhuMnZjdjVfMTY1Y3FnaGpqY3Y&hl=en_GB (A Google Docs presentation with ideas for teaching Internet safety in the classroom)
Center for Safe and Responsible Internet Use: http://www.cyberbully.org
Common Sense Media and CyberSmart Curriculum: http://cybersmartcurriculum.org/lessonsbygrade
Computer Crime & Intellectual Property Section—United States Department of Justice: http://www.justice.gov/criminal/cybercrime/cyberethics.htm
Cyber Citizen Partnership: http://www.cybercitizenship.org
"Cyber Ethics," Norton by Symantec: http://us.norton.com/library/familyresource/article.jsp?aid=pr_cyberethics (Teaching your children acceptable behavior on the Internet)
Digizen: http://digizen.org
Federal Trade Commission: http://bulkorder.ftc.gov (Internet safety booklets and bookmarks)
Internet 4 Classrooms: http://www.internet4classrooms.com/character_ed.htm#bully
iSafe: http://www.isafe.org
Netsmartz: http://www.netsmartz.org/Parents
Own Your Space: A Security Book for Teens, 100 Page Press: http://100pagepress.com (A free ebook on Internet safety)
Web Wise Kids: http://www.webwisekids.org/classroom_resources
WiredSafety: http://www.wiredsafety.org

Ways to Avoid Risks Involved with Using Networking Sites

As students shift from sharing their learning in the classroom to discussing their ideas online, they move from a very controlled environment to one where anyone—

friend or foe—can connect with them. Every student is different, and complete open access to the Internet may not be the most appropriate option for every student, so there are some precautions to take. When planning lessons and units, you should review the sites students will use in advance. You should also consider creating a learning outline or guide for students with directions and direct links to sites. This helps keep the lesson on track and the students focused. When doing searches, there are safe search sites such as KidsClick (http://www.kidsclick.org), which is great for elementary students and also sorts by reading level. For secondary students, Google allows you to do a safe search by setting preferences to "Use Strict Filtering."

There are many educational versions of similar public networking sites, which ensures that inappropriate materials will not pop up. Ning (http://education.ning.com) is one example of a way to use educational social networks similar to Facebook or Myspace without the risk of predators or inappropriate material. The Flat Classroom Project (http://flatclassroomproject.ning.com) is one example where educators have built educational networking sites specifically for use in class and home assignments. Not only does this allow for educationally relevant communication for students in the classroom, but it also allows students to interact with other students in classrooms both in the United States and abroad. Thus, students around the world can communicate and learn from each other. Other examples of sites with educational versions include the following: Scholarpedia (http://www.scholarpedia.org) instead of Wikipedia; TeacherTube (http://teachertube.com) instead of YouTube; and Glogster Edu (http://edu.glogster.com) instead of Glogster. In addition, Edmodo (http://www.edmodo.com) is a networking site similar to Facebook that allows students to share files, hand in assignments, and connect to classmates and teachers.

3

Media Sharing Sites
in the Classroom

Why Use Media Sharing Sites?

Media sharing sites are some of the most popular of all networking sites. One of the biggest, YouTube, draws millions of viewers every day. YouTube is one of the best places to go to learn about a new technology. Users are constantly posting videos showing step-by-step directions for every technology you could imagine. You can see some truly disturbing, inappropriate material on YouTube, and it is a great way to waste tons of time. But mixed into all those entertaining videos on YouTube you will find just as many videos that are available to inform and educate. Watching videos improves listening skills while creating videos improves communication skills—verbal and written. As budgets continue to be slashed, YouTube can supplement lessons through free videos that offer learning opportunities from around the world. Of course, students should be monitored on YouTube, but the site should not be completely blocked from access. Teachers are trained professionals who should be trusted to use YouTube appropriately to meet educational objectives in their classrooms.

Besides YouTube, the most widely used media sharing sites include Flickr, Wikimedia Commons, and Glogster. Media sharing sites are popular for many reasons: most are free, they are easy to access, and people love watching videos and listening to audio. The real beauty of media sharing sites is that they are not just about consuming, but rather about creating and posting your own work. Not too long ago, making a video or audio recording required expensive video equipment and software, but that is no longer the case. With a very inexpensive Web camera or microphone and free software, your students could create the next great video or music sensation.

Media sharing sites can be very useful for library public relations when they are used to communicate with patrons about services, resources, and events available in the library. It is a good idea to constantly take pictures of patrons in action, unique displays, and events happening in the library, and then make those pictures available on networking sites. A good site to share pictures is Flickr because you can then link the slideshows of pictures of the library to your library website or blog. Just make sure you have the patrons' permission (or their guardians' permission if they are minors) to post their pictures if they are recognizable in the image. These pictures will allow patrons to feel ownership because *their* picture is on the library site, will allow people who do not frequent the library in person to see the wonderful activities and events that are taking place so that they plan a visit to get in on the action themselves, and can also serve as documentation of resources in the library in case of some disaster or burglary.

Media Sharing Site Lesson Plans

The following lesson plans incorporate media sharing sites such as YouTube, Flickr, and Glogster to share pictures, videos, and audio recordings. The three stages of lesson plans allow anyone to incorporate the idea of media sharing networking sites into their classroom regardless of technology restrictions.

Stage One: Promotional Book Poster Lesson Plan

Overview

After reading a book, students will create a promotional poster for their book. Stage one users have limited access to technology or the Internet, so technology is usually utilized by the teacher for demonstration and display purposes. To overcome these technology obstacles, this particular lesson requires the teacher or librarian to use the technology for production and the students to only view the technology through a teacher presentation.

Common Core State Standards

CC.5–8.L.3 Students use knowledge of language and its conventions when writing, speaking, reading, or listening.

CC.7.L.3.a Students choose language that expresses ideas precisely and concisely, recognizing and eliminating wordiness and redundancy.

CC.9–12.L.3 Students apply knowledge of language to understand how language functions in different contexts, to make effective choices for meaning or style, and to comprehend more fully when reading or listening.

CC.5.R.L.2 Students determine a theme of a story, drama, or poem from details in the text, including how characters in a story or drama respond to challenges or how the speaker in a poem reflects upon a topic; summarize the text.

CC.6.R.L.2 Students determine a theme or central idea of a text and how it is conveyed through particular details; provide a summary of the text distinct from personal opinions or judgments.

CC.7.R.L.2 Students determine a theme or central idea of a text and analyze its development over the course of the text; provide an objective summary of the text.

CC.8.R.L.2 Students determine a theme or central idea of a text and analyze its development over the course of the text, including its relationship to the characters, setting, and plot; provide an objective summary of the text.

CC.9–10.R.L.2 Students determine a theme or central idea of a text and analyze in detail its development over the course of the text, including how it emerges and is shaped and refined by specific details; provide an objective summary of the text.

CC.11–12.R.L.2 Determine two or more themes or central ideas of a text and analyze their development over the course of the text, including how they interact and build on one another to produce a complex account; provide an objective summary of the text.

Terms to Know

Audio—Audible content with file format extensions that include mp3, wav, mid, au, snd, ra, rmi, mid, aif, aifc, aiff, m3u, and ram.

Blog—A website that contains a writer's thoughts, reflections, comments, and often hyperlinks. The word *blog* is a shortened form of *Web log*.

Creative Commons—Licensed content such as videos, images, and music that are made available to the public for free legal sharing, reuse, and, depending on the type of license, remixing.

Glog—An interactive poster created using the Glogster website (http://www.glogster.com). Glogs can incorporate photographs, images, graphics, video files, and audio files.

Glogger—Someone who creates a Glog.

Image—Two-dimensional picture content with file format extensions that include jpg, jpe, jpeg, bmp, gif, cod, ief, jiff, png, svg, tif, tiff, ras, cmx, ico, pnm, pbm, pgm, ppm, rgb, xbm, xpm, and xwd.

Multimedia—Mixing printed words, video, sound, and pictures in one place, such as videos that appear in the middle of webpages.

Podcast—An audio recording available online. The word *podcasting* is a combination of the words *iPod* and *broadcasting*.

QR code—Stands for "quick response barcode." QR codes are two-dimensional barcodes that can be read by dedicated QR scanners or smartphones. These barcodes can encode URLs, text, phone numbers, and more.

Script—The written part, including dialogue, of a comic book, graphic novel, play, movie, or television show.

Smartphone—A wireless phone that functions similar to a mini computer, allowing the user to access the Internet, run complicated applications, record video and audio, take pictures, and much more.

SMS—Stands for "short message service." This service enables cellular phone users to send and receive text messages. SMS is also used to refer to the actual text messages.

Storyboard—Panels of sketches that show the plans for the scenes and actions for a comic book, graphic novel, movie, or television show.

Terms to Know

URL—Uniform resource locator, more commonly known as the Web address.

Video—Content that represents images in motion. File format extensions include avi, mp4, mpe, mpa, mpeg, mpg, mpv2, mov, qt, lsf, lsx, asf, asr, asx, and movie.

Vlog—A video blog.

Vodcast—A video podcast.

Networking Sites to Know

Creative Commons (http://search.creativecommons.org) is a website that offers a convenient way to search one website to access Creative Commons licensed images, videos, and other media that can be found on Wikimedia Commons, Flickr, Google Web, Google Images, Blip.tv, Jamendo, and Spinxpree websites.

Flickr (http://www.flickr.com) is a website that allows users to upload, organize, share, and find images and videos. The site has over five billion images already uploaded. Users who sign up for a free account are allowed to upload 300 MB of images a month and two videos.

Jamendo (http://www.jamendo.com/en) is a website to upload, organize, share, stream, and download royalty-free music.

TeacherTube (http://teachertube.com) is a website that provides a safe online community for sharing instructional videos.

Wikimedia Commons (http://commons.wikimedia.org) is a media sharing website that provides public domain and freely-licensed educational videos, images, and audio files.

YouTube (http://www.youtube.com/) is a website to watch and share originally created videos.

Other Websites Used in the Lessons

Animoto (http://animoto.com) is a tool for online video creation. Students simply upload a selection of still images or video clips, then select or upload a soundtrack for their video. Animoto's program handles all processing, including editing, of the video. Teachers can apply for a free Animoto for Education (http://animoto.com/education) account, which grants students free access to features that the service normally charges for.

Resources Needed

Library or classroom book

Poster board, paper, glue, markers/crayons, pens/pencils, scissors, and magazines to cut pictures from

Networking Media Used

YouTube (http://www.youtube.com), TeacherTube (http://teachertube.com), and Wikimedia Commons (http://commons.wikimedia.org) to show book trailers, movie trailers, and movie promotional posters

Flickr (http://www.flickr.com) to share pictures of the students' finished products

Procedures

Students will chose a library book to read on their reading level (or this lesson can be used for a required classroom reading assignment). This lesson requires teachers and librarians to find or create book trailers to share with the students. Thousands of book trailers are available on many sites, such as TeacherTube and YouTube. The teacher and librarian will show several examples of appropriate grade level book trailers and then brainstorm with the students the elements that make a quality book trailer—plot introduced but not completely revealed, interesting, good selection of pictures, music or sound is appropriate, makes you want to check out the book, and so on. Other discussion topics will follow viewing the trailers, such as how the book trailer compares to movie trailers that students have seen (movie trailers can also be found on YouTube). The teacher should guide the discussion by asking if students have ever seen promotional movie posters that encourage people to watch a movie. If students cannot remember seeing such posters, the teacher can show examples on the media sharing site Wikimedia Commons by typing in the search term "movie posters." Discussion should include what elements make a quality promotional movie poster—plot introduced but not completely revealed, interesting, good selection of pictures, makes you want to see the movie, and so on.

After reading their books, students will create a promotional poster on their book. The students will organize their ideas by summarizing the book through writing four brief statements that include these elements:

1. Identification of the main character(s)
2. Outline of the major story plot
3. Identification of the setting and time period of the story
4. Identification of the major themes of the story

Students will then create a poster to promote the book by drawing or pasting pictures that represent key elements from the story and providing text that hooks a reader. The posters should demonstrate a scene from the book, communicate a theme, feature a symbol, or include some of each. The poster must also state that the book is available in the library (for example "Check out this enthralling book now available in your library"). The posters can be hung in the library, in the classroom, or in prominent places around the building for everyone to see. The teacher or librarian can also take a digital picture of each poster to post on a media sharing site, such as Flickr, or the school website. A rubric given before the project is started will keep students on track and allow students to understand how they will be graded (see following rubric).

Stage Two: Glogster Edu Promotional Book Poster Lesson Plan

Overview

The stage one lesson can easily be carried into a stage two lesson plan by completing the poster on Glogster Edu (http://edu.glogster.com) instead of on poster board. A stage two lesson would require students to use the computer to create the interactive Glog using text and pictures they find on the Internet. The educational site is a stage two lesson because students cannot see content from the regular Glogster site and all Glogs made by students on the teacher page are private.

> ### Other Websites Used in the Lessons
>
> **Blip.tv** (http://blip.tv) is a website that features original Web series from professional and up-and-coming producers.
>
> **Glogster** (http://www.glogster.com) is a website to create a Glog (see definition in "Terms to Know").
>
> **Glogster Edu** (http://edu.glogster.com) is a website to create a private Glog (see definition in "Terms to Know") on a teacher's page. The educational site does not allow users to view public Glogs.
>
> **JayCut** (http://jaycut.com) is a tool for online video creation. JayCut lets users mix multiple tracks, combine clips, create voiceovers, and add transitions between scenes. There are two ways that schools can use JayCut: users can register for a free account to create and save their files on the website, or the program can be installed on a school's local server.
>
> **One True Media** (http://www.onetruemedia.com) is a tool for online video creation. Students simply upload a selection of still images or video clips, then select or upload a soundtrack for their video. One True Media's program handles all processing, including editing, of the video.
>
> **Quikqr** (http://quikqr.com) is a free website that has both a QR code generator and a QR code reader.
>
> **SpinXpress** (http://spinXpress.com) is a website to find Creative Commons video, image, and audio files.

Information and Technology Literacy Standards

NETS5.a Students advocate and practice safe, legal, and responsible use of information and technology.

NETS5.b Students exhibit a positive attitude toward using technology that supports collaboration, learning, and productivity.

NETS5.c Students demonstrate personal responsibility for lifelong learning.

NETS5.d Students exhibit leadership for digital citizenship.

Common Core State Standards

CC.5–8.L.3 Students use knowledge of language and its conventions when writing, speaking, reading, or listening.

CC.7.L.3.a Students choose language that expresses ideas precisely and concisely, recognizing and eliminating wordiness and redundancy.

CC.9–12.L.3 Students apply knowledge of language to understand how language functions in different contexts, to make effective choices for meaning or style, and to comprehend more fully when reading or listening.

TABLE 3.1   Promotional Book Poster Rubric

Elements	Exemplary 3	Satisfactory but lacking in some areas 2	Needs improvement 1	Score
Book hook	Text on the poster clearly and accurately represents the main ideas of the book with sufficient detail to hook a reader. All details of the book are summarized without giving the climax or ending away.	Text on the poster is not a completely accurate representation of the main ideas of the book, not clearly presented, or summarized in a way that spoils part of the story for a reader by giving away too many details.	Text on the poster is incomplete, off topic, inaccurate, or summarized in a way that spoils part of the story for a reader by giving away too many details.	
Organization	The poster is attractive to look at. The poster is neat and organized in design and layout.	The poster is acceptably attractive though it may be a bit unorganized in places or look a little messy.	The organization of the poster and/or its design makes it distracting to look at or unattractive.	
Pictures	Pictures demonstrate a scene from the book, communicate a theme, feature a symbol, or include some of each.	Pictures are not the best quality or it is hard to understand exactly what they represent.	Pictures are missing, pictures are very poor quality, or pictures seem random and do not represent the book.	
Mechanics	All text is legible and easy to read. There are no grammatical and/or mechanical mistakes on the poster.	Most of the text is legible and easy to read. There are one or two grammatical and/or mechanical mistakes on the poster.	The text is illegible or otherwise hard to read. There are three or more grammatical and/or mechanical mistakes on the poster.	
Overall construction	Book title and author are clearly identified. All the space on the poster board is used efficiently. Poster shows creativity and originality. Poster entices people to check out the book. Poster clearly states that the book can be checked out from the library.	Book title is clearly identified but author is not. Most of the space on the poster board is used efficiently. Poster shows some creativity and originality but needs improvement. Poster encourages the reader to get the book but does not state that it is available in the library.	Book title and author are not clearly identified. The space on the poster board is either very cluttered or there is too much empty space. Poster lacks creativity and originality. The poster does not encourage other people to want to the read the book. Poster does not state that the book can be checked out from the library.	

Total score (out of 15)

CC.5.R.L.2 Students determine a theme of a story, drama, or poem from details in the text, including how characters in a story or drama respond to challenges or how the speaker in a poem reflects upon a topic; summarize the text.

CC.6.R.L.2 Students determine a theme or central idea of a text and how it is conveyed through particular details; provide a summary of the text distinct from personal opinions or judgments.

CC.7.R.L.2 Students determine a theme or central idea of a text and analyze its development over the course of the text; provide an objective summary of the text.

CC.8.R.L.2 Students determine a theme or central idea of a text and analyze its development over the course of the text, including its relationship to the characters, setting, and plot; provide an objective summary of the text.

CC.9–10.R.L.2 Students determine a theme or central idea of a text and analyze in detail its development over the course of the text, including how it emerges and is shaped and refined by specific details; provide an objective summary of the text.

CC.11–12.R.L.2 Determine two or more themes or central ideas of a text and analyze their development over the course of the text, including how they interact and build on one another to produce a complex account; provide an objective summary of the text.

CC.6.S.L.5 Students include multimedia components (e.g., graphics, image, music, sound) and visual displays in presentations to clarify information.

CC.7.S.L.5 Students include multimedia components and visual displays in presentations to clarify claims and findings and emphasize salient points.

CC.8.S.L.5 Students include multimedia components and visual displays into presentations to clarify information, strengthen claims and evidence, and add interest.

Resources Needed

Library or classroom book

Computers with Internet access

Networking Media Used

YouTube (http://www.youtube.com), TeacherTube (http://teachertube.com), and Wikimedia Commons (http://commons.wikimedia.org) to show book trailers, movie trailers, and movie promotional posters

Creative Commons (http://search.creativecommons.org) website to find images to use on the Glog

Glogster Edu (http://edu.glogster.com)

Quikqr (http://quikqr.com) is a free website that has both a QR code generator and a QR code reader

Procedures

Students will chose a library book to read on their reading level (or this lesson can be used for a required classroom reading assignment). This lesson requires teachers and librarians to find or create book trailers to share with the students. Thousands of book trailers are available on many sites, such as TeacherTube and YouTube, and examples can be found on my blog. The teacher and librarian will show several examples of appropriate grade level book trailers and then brainstorm with the students the elements that make a quality book trailer—plot introduced but not completely revealed, interesting, good selection of pictures, music or sound is appropriate, makes you want to check out the book, and so on. Other discussion topics will follow viewing the trailers, such as how the book trailer compares to movie trailers that students have seen (movie trailers can also be found on YouTube). The teacher should guide the discussion by asking if students have ever seen promotional movie posters that encourage people to watch a movie. If students cannot remember seeing such posters, the teacher can show examples on the media sharing site Wikimedia Commons by typing in the search term "movie posters." Discussion should include what elements make a quality promotional movie poster—plot introduced but not completely revealed, interesting, good selection of pictures, makes you want to see the movie, and so on.

After reading their chosen library books, students will create a promotional Glog for their book. The students will organize their ideas by summarizing the book through writing four brief statements that include these elements:

1. Identification of the main character(s)

2. Outline of the major story plot

3. Identification of the setting and time period of the story

4. Identification of the major themes of the story

The teacher or librarian will set up accounts for each of their students on Glogster Edu. The librarian will teach technology lessons on how to create a Glog as well as how to search for pictures and cite sources. Students will then create a Glog to promote the book by finding Creative Commons images, videos, and audio recordings on the Internet (or create their own) that represent key elements from the story and providing text that hooks a reader. At least one picture, one video, and one audio recording are required on the Glog. The Glog should demonstrate a scene from the book, communicate a theme, feature a symbol, or include some of each. The Glog must also state that the book is available in the library (for example "Check out this dramatic read now available in your library"). Once the Glogs are created, they can be embedded on the teacher's website. All Glogs will be available for the teacher and classmates to see but not the general public. A rubric given before the project is started will keep students on track and allow students to understand how they will be graded (see rubric in the stage three lesson).

Extension: QR Codes

Once the students have created their Glogs, a QR code can be generated and glued to the inside cover of the book. By scanning these codes with their smartphone, patrons could view the promotional poster to decide if they want to check out the book. See this example Glog created on Glogster Edu for the book *Shiver* by Maggie Stiefvater (http://gamedia.edu.glogster.com/glogexample):

Free websites can be used to generate a QR code within seconds. This QR code was created by Quikqr (http://quikqr.com), a site that has both a free QR code generator and a free QR code reader. A QR code reader app must be installed on smartphones in order to actually scan the bar code. The short, simple directions for generating a QR code using Quikqr are as follows:

1. Go to Quikqr at http://quikqr.com.

2. Enter a URL or text that you want the QR code to direct users to.

3. Hit the "Generate Code" button.

Once the code is generated, it can be saved by clicking the "Save QR Code as a PNG image" button or by entering your email address to have it sent directly to you. Once the code is saved, it can be printed and displayed anywhere—on books, on bulletin boards, on websites, and so forth.

Stage Three: Glogster Promotional Book Poster Lesson Plan

Overview

The stage two lesson can easily be carried into a stage three lesson plan by completing the poster on Glogster's public site (http://www.glogster.com) instead of on the private educational site. A stage three lesson would require students to access all the networking sites themselves to view trailers and pictures as well as view example Glogs on the Glogster site.

Information and Technology Literacy Standards

NETS5.a Students advocate and practice safe, legal, and responsible use of information and technology.

NETS5.b Students exhibit a positive attitude toward using technology that supports collaboration, learning, and productivity.

NETS5.c Students demonstrate personal responsibility for lifelong learning.

NETS5.d Students exhibit leadership for digital citizenship.

Common Core State Standards

CC.5–8.L.3 Students use knowledge of language and its conventions when writing, speaking, reading, or listening.

CC.7.L.3.a Students choose language that expresses ideas precisely and concisely, recognizing and eliminating wordiness and redundancy.

CC.9–12.L.3 Students apply knowledge of language to understand how language functions in different contexts, to make effective choices for meaning or style, and to comprehend more fully when reading or listening.

CC.6.S.L.5 Students include multimedia components (e.g., graphics, image, music, sound) and visual displays in presentations to clarify information.

CC.7.S.L.5 Students include multimedia components and visual displays in presentations to clarify claims and findings and emphasize salient points.

CC.8.S.L.5 Students include multimedia components and visual displays into presentations to clarify information, strengthen claims and evidence, and add interest.

CC.9–12.S.L.5 Students make strategic use of digital media (e.g., textual, graphical, audio, visual, and interactive elements) in presentations to enhance understanding of findings, reasoning, and evidence and to add interest.

CC.5.R.L.2 Students determine a theme of a story, drama, or poem from details in the text, including how characters in a story or drama respond to challenges or how the speaker in a poem reflects upon a topic; summarize the text.

CC.6.R.L.2 Students determine a theme or central idea of a text and how it is conveyed through particular details; provide a summary of the text distinct from personal opinions or judgments.

CC.7.R.L.2 Students determine a theme or central idea of a text and analyze its development over the course of the text; provide an objective summary of the text.

CC.8.R.L.2 Students determine a theme or central idea of a text and analyze its development over the course of the text, including its relationship to the characters, setting, and plot; provide an objective summary of the text.

CC.9–10.R.L.2 Students determine a theme or central idea of a text and analyze in detail its development over the course of the text, including how it emerges and is shaped and refined by specific details; provide an objective summary of the text.

CC.11–12.R.L.2 Determine two or more themes or central ideas of a text and analyze their development over the course of the text, including how they interact and build on one another to produce a complex account; provide an objective summary of the text.

Resources Needed

Library or classroom book

Computers with Internet access

Networking Media Used

YouTube (http://www.youtube.com), TeacherTube (http://teachertube.com), and Wikimedia Commons (http://commons.wikimedia.org) to show book trailers, movie trailers, and movie promotional posters

Creative Commons (http://search.creativecommons.org) to find images to use on Glog

---

Glogster website (http://glogster.com)

Quikqr (http://quikqr.com) is a free website that has both a QR code generator and a QR code reader

Procedures

Students will chose a library book to read on their reading level (or this lesson can be used for a required classroom reading assignment). This lesson requires students to search for examples of book trailers, movie trailers, promotional movie posters, and example Glogs. The students will start by searching for and comparing book trailers and movie trailers. The teacher and librarian will then brainstorm with the students the elements that make a quality book trailer or movie trailer—plot introduced but not completely revealed, interesting, good selection of pictures, music or sound is appropriate, makes you want to check out the book or see the movie, and so on. Students will then search the Internet for examples of promotional movie trailers and examples of Glogs. Discussions should follow that include what elements make a quality promotional movie poster and a good Glog—plot introduced but not completely revealed, interesting, good selection of pictures, makes you want to see the movie, and so on.

After reading their books, students will create a promotional Glog for their book. The students will organize their ideas by summarizing the book through writing four brief statements that include these elements:

1. Identification of the main character(s)

2. Outline of the major story plot

3. Identification of the setting and time period of the story

4. Identification of the major themes of the story

The librarian will teach technology lessons on how to create a Glog as well as how to search for pictures, videos and audio recordings and cite sources. The students will set up their own accounts on Glogster's public site.

Students will then create a Glog to promote the book by finding Creative Commons images, videos, and audio recordings on the Internet (or create their own) that represent key elements from the story and providing text that hooks a reader. At least one picture, one video, and one audio recording are required on the Glog. The Glog should demonstrate a scene from the book, communicate a theme, feature a symbol, or include some of each. The Glog must also state that the book is available in the library (for example "Check out this gripping read now available in your library"). All Glogs will then be made available for the general public to view. A rubric given before the project is started will keep students on track and allow students to understand how they will be graded (see the rubric at the end of this lesson plan).

Extension: QR Codes

Once the students have created their Glogs, a QR code can be generated and glued to the inside cover of the book. By scanning these codes with their smartphone, patrons could view the promotional poster to decide if they want to check out the book. See this example Glog for the book *The Hunger Games* by Suzanne Collins (http://galibrary.glogster.com/hunger-games):

Free websites can be used to generate a QR code within seconds. This QR code was created by Quikqr (http://quikqr.com), a site that has both a free QR code

generator and a free QR code reader. A QR code reader app must be installed on smartphones in order to actually scan the bar code. The short, simple directions for generating a QR code using Quikqr are as follows:

1. Go to Quikqr at http://quikqr.com.

2. Enter a URL or text that you want the QR code to direct users to.

3. Hit the "Generate Code" button.

Once the code is generated, it can be saved by clicking the "Save QR Code as a PNG image" button or by entering your email address to have it sent directly to you. Once the code is saved, it can be printed and displayed anywhere—on books, on bulletin boards, on websites, and so forth.

Lesson Plans Adapted for Other Subjects

Use subject-area learning standards to summarize one concept, from an informational textbook reading, in the form of a poster.

Use science learning standards to create a promotional poster advertising one of the elements from the periodic table.

See the author's blog (http://networkedlibrary.wordpress.com, password "library") for links to Glog examples for both these lesson plan adaptations.

TABLE 3.2   Book Glog Rubric

Elements	Exemplary 3	Satisfactory but lacking in some areas 2	Needs improvement 1	Score
Book hook	Text on the Glog clearly and accurately represents the main plot of the book with sufficient detail to hook a reader. All details of the book are provided without giving the climax or ending away.	Text on the Glog is not a completely accurate representation of the main plot of the book, not clearly presented, or presented in a way that spoils part of the story for a reader by giving away too many details.	Text on the Glog is incomplete, off topic, inaccurate, or presented in a way that spoils part of the story for a reader by giving away too many details.	
Organization	The Glog is attractive to look at. The Glog is neat and organized in design and layout.	The Glog is acceptably attractive though it may be a bit unorganized in places or look a little messy.	The organization of the Glog and/or its design makes it distracting to look at or unattractive.	
Pictures, videos, and audio recordings	There is at least one picture, one video, and one audio recording present on the Glog. Pictures, videos, and audio recordings demonstrate a scene from the book, communicate a theme, feature a symbol, or include some of each.	One of the three required elements is missing. Required elements include: one picture, one video, and one audio recording. Pictures, videos, and audio recordings are not the best quality or it is hard to understand exactly what they represent.	Pictures, videos, and audio recordings are missing or are very poor quality. Pictures, videos, and audio recordings seem random and do not represent the book.	
Mechanics	There are no grammatical and/or mechanical mistakes on the Glog.	There are one or two grammatical and/or mechanical mistakes on the Glog.	There are three or more grammatical and/or mechanical mistakes on the Glog.	
Overall construction	Book title and author are clearly identified. Glog shows creativity and originality. Glog entices people to check out the book. Glog clearly states that the book can be checked out from the library.	Book title is clearly identified but author is not. Glog shows some creativity and originality but needs improvement. Glog encourages the reader to get the book but does not state that it is available in the library.	Book title and author are not clearly identified. Glog lacks creativity and originality. The Glog does not encourage other people to want to the read the book. Glog does not state that the book can be checked out from the library.	

Total score (out of 15)

Stage One: Book Review Storyboard/Script Lesson Plan

Overview

Students will read a book and then write a storyboard or script to be used as a book review to encourage others to check out that book. Students will post the storyboard/script in the library, in the classroom, or in prominent places around the building for everyone to see. Pictures of the finished products can also be digitally photographed and shared on a media sharing website, such as Flickr. Stage one users have limited access to technology or the Internet, so technology is usually utilized by the teacher for demonstration and display purposes. To overcome these technology obstacles, this particular lesson requires the teacher or librarian to use the technology for production and the students to only view the technology through a teacher presentation.

Common Core State Standards

CC.5–8.L.3 Students use knowledge of language and its conventions when writing, speaking, reading, or listening.

CC.7.L.3.a Students choose language that expresses ideas precisely and concisely, recognizing and eliminating wordiness and redundancy.

CC.9–12.L.3 Students apply knowledge of language to understand how language functions in different contexts, to make effective choices for meaning or style, and to comprehend more fully when reading or listening.

CC.5.R.L.2 Students determine a theme of a story, drama, or poem from details in the text, including how characters in a story or drama respond to challenges or how the speaker in a poem reflects upon a topic; summarize the text.

CC.6.R.L.2 Students determine a theme or central idea of a text and how it is conveyed through particular details; provide a summary of the text distinct from personal opinions or judgments.

CC.7.R.L.2 Students determine a theme or central idea of a text and analyze its development over the course of the text; provide an objective summary of the text.

CC.8.R.L.2 Students determine a theme or central idea of a text and analyze its development over the course of the text, including its relationship to the characters, setting, and plot; provide an objective summary of the text.

CC.9–10.R.L.2 Students determine a theme or central idea of a text and analyze in detail its development over the course of the text, including how it emerges and is shaped and refined by specific details; provide an objective summary of the text.

CC.11–12.R.L.2 Determine two or more themes or central ideas of a text and analyze their development over the course of the text, including how they interact and build on one another to produce a complex account; provide an objective summary of the text.

Resources Needed

Library or classroom book

Paper, glue, markers/crayons, pens/pencils, scissors, and magazines to cut pictures from

Networking Media Used

YouTube (http://www.youtube.com), TeacherTube (http://teachertube.com), and Wikimedia Commons (http://commons.wikimedia.org) to show book and movie trailers

Flickr (http://www.flickr.com) to share pictures of the students' finished products

Procedures

Students will chose a library book to read on their reading level (or this lesson can be used for a required classroom reading assignment). This lesson requires the teacher and/or the librarian to find or create book trailers to share with the students. Thousands of book trailers are available on many sites, such as TeacherTube and YouTube, and several book trailers created by the author are included in the following lesson plans. The teacher and/or librarian will show several examples of appropriate grade level book trailers and then brainstorm with the students the elements that make a quality book trailer—plot introduced but not completely revealed, interesting, good selection of pictures, music or sound is appropriate, makes you want to check out the book, and so on. Other discussion topics will follow viewing the trailers, such as how the book trailer compares to movie trailers that students have seen (movie trailers can also be found on YouTube) and how all trailers should start as a script.

After reading a book, students will summarize the book by writing a storyboard or script that includes these elements:

1. Identification of the main character(s)

2. Outline of the major story plot

TABLE 3.3   Book Review Storyboard/Script Handout

Name: _____

Date: _____

Book Review Storyboard/Script

Slide 1	*Slide 2*	*Slide 3*
Text/Picture:	Text/Picture:	Text/Picture:

Slide 4	*Slide 5*	*Slide 6*
Text/Picture:	Text/Picture:	Text/Picture:

Slide 7	*Slide 8*	*Slide 9*
Text/Picture:	Text/Picture:	Text/Picture:

3. Identification of the setting and time period of the story

4. Identification of the major themes of the story

Students will then create a storyboard/script to promote the book by drawing or pasting pictures that represent these key elements from the story beside the text that they have written (see Tables 3.3 and 3.4). The storyboard/script must have at least nine panels. Panels can demonstrate a scene from the book, communicate a theme, feature a symbol, use literary devices, or include some of each. The storyboard/script must also state that the book is available in the library (for example, "Grab this great read at your library"). The storyboard/script can be hung in the

TABLE 3.4 Book Review Storyboard/Script Example

Name: ___A. Student___

Date: _September 1, 2011_

Book Review Storyboard/Script

Slide 1	Slide 2	Slide 3
Text/Picture: #1 New York Times bestseller *The Hunger Games*	Text/Picture: Picture of *The Hunger Games* book jacket	Text/Picture: By Suzanne Collins and picture of author

Slide 4	Slide 5	Slide 6
Text/Picture: In a not too distant future, a lottery determines who will fight to the death in the brutal Hunger Games.	Text/Picture: Picture of two people fighting	Text/Picture: Sixteen-year-old Katniss volunteers to participate in the games to keep her young sister safe.

Slide 7	Slide 8	Slide 9
Text/Picture: Picture of two girls together	Text/Picture: Every member of this future society watches every second of the televised games to see which of the 24 participants will survive and who will be killed before their eyes.	Text/Picture: Check out this intense read at your library to see if Katniss will be declared the winner of this cruel game.

library, in the classroom, or in prominent places around the building for everyone to see. The teacher or librarian can also take a digital picture of each storyboard/script to post on a media sharing site, such as Flickr, or the school website. A rubric given before the project is started will keep students on track and allow students to understand how they will be graded (see the rubric at the end of this lesson plan).

TABLE 3.5   Book Review Storyboard/Script Rubric

Elements	Exemplary 3	Satisfactory but lacking in some areas 2	Needs improvement 1	Score
Book summary	Storyboard/script clearly and accurately summarizes the book with sufficient detail but without giving the climax or ending away. Storyboard/script contains a minimum of all four of these elements: identification of the main character(s), outline of the major story plot, identification of the setting and/or time period of the story, and identification of the major themes of the story.	Book summary presented in the storyboard/script is not completely accurate, not clearly presented, or presented in a way that spoils part of the story for a reader by giving away too many details. Storyboard/script is missing one or two of these elements: identification of the main character(s), outline of the major story plot, identification of the setting and/or time period of the story, and identification of the major themes of the story.	Storyboard/script is incomplete, off topic, inaccurate, or presented in a way that spoils part of the story for a reader by giving away too many details. Storyboard/script is missing three or four of these elements: identification of the main character(s), outline of the major story plot, identification of the setting and/or time period of the story, and identification of the major themes of the story.	
Organization	The storyboard/script is neat and organized in design and layout. Story is easy to follow.	The storyboard/script a bit unorganized in places or looks a little messy.	The organization and/or design of the storyboard/script makes it distracting or hard to follow.	
Mechanics	All text is legible and easy to read. There are no grammatical and/or mechanical mistakes.	Most of the text is legible and easy to read. There are one or two grammatical and/or mechanical mistakes.	The text is illegible and hard to read. There are three or more grammatical and/or mechanical mistakes.	
Overall construction	Book title and author are clearly identified. Storyboard/script shows creativity and originality. Storyboard/script entices people to check out the book. Storyboard/script clearly states that the book can be checked out from the library.	Book title is clearly identified but author is not. Storyboard/script shows some creativity and originality but needs improvement. Storyboard/script encourages the reader to get the book but does not state that it is available in the library.	Book title and author are not clearly identified. Storyboard/script lacks creativity and originality. Storyboard/script does not encourage other people to want to read the book. Storyboard/script does not state that the book can be checked out from the library.	

Total score (out of 12)

Stage Two: Thirty-Second Book Trailer Lesson Plan

Overview

The stage one lesson can easily be carried into a stage two lesson plan by turning the storyboard/script created in the stage one lesson into a short 30-second book trailer. A stage two lesson would require students to use the computer to create a short 30-second book trailer using text and pictures they find on the Internet. Students will then share the book trailers with the entire class.

Information and Technology Literacy Standards

NETS5.a Students advocate and practice safe, legal, and responsible use of information and technology.

NETS5.b Students exhibit a positive attitude toward using technology that supports collaboration, learning, and productivity.

NETS5.c Students demonstrate personal responsibility for lifelong learning.

NETS5.d Students exhibit leadership for digital citizenship.

Common Core State Standards

CC.5–8.L.3 Students use knowledge of language and its conventions when writing, speaking, reading, or listening.

CC.7.L.3.a Students choose language that expresses ideas precisely and concisely, recognizing and eliminating wordiness and redundancy.

CC.9–12.L.3 Students apply knowledge of language to understand how language functions in different contexts, to make effective choices for meaning or style, and to comprehend more fully when reading or listening.

CC.5.R.L.2 Students determine a theme of a story, drama, or poem from details in the text, including how characters in a story or drama respond to challenges or how the speaker in a poem reflects upon a topic; summarize the text.

CC.6.R.L.2 Students determine a theme or central idea of a text and how it is conveyed through particular details; provide a summary of the text distinct from personal opinions or judgments.

CC.7.R.L.2 Students determine a theme or central idea of a text and analyze its development over the course of the text; provide an objective summary of the text.

CC.8.R.L.2 Students determine a theme or central idea of a text and analyze its development over the course of the text, including its relationship to the characters, setting, and plot; provide an objective summary of the text.

CC.9–10.R.L.2 Students determine a theme or central idea of a text and analyze in detail its development over the course of the text, including how it emerges and is shaped and refined by specific details; provide an objective summary of the text.

CC.11–12.R.L.2 Determine two or more themes or central ideas of a text and analyze their development over the course of the text, including how they interact and build on one another to produce a complex account; provide an objective summary of the text.

CC.6.S.L.5 Students include multimedia components (e.g., graphics, image, music, sound) and visual displays in presentations to clarify information.

CC.7.S.L.5 Students include multimedia components and visual displays in presentations to clarify claims and findings and emphasize salient points.

CC.8.S.L.5 Students include multimedia components and visual displays into presentations to clarify information, strengthen claims and evidence, and add interest.

CC.9–12.S.L.5 Students make strategic use of digital media (e.g., textual, graphical, audio, visual, and interactive elements) in presentations to enhance understanding of findings, reasoning, and evidence and to add interest.

Resources Needed

Library or classroom book

Storyboard/script from stage one lesson plan

Computers with Internet access

Networking Media Used

YouTube (http://www.youtube.com), TeacherTube (http://teachertube.com), and Wikimedia Commons (http://commons.wikimedia.org) to show book and movie trailers

Creative Commons (http://search.creativecommons.org) to find images

One True Media (http://www.onetruemedia.com) or Animoto (http://animoto.com) to produce the book trailer

Quikqr (http://quikqr.com) is a free website that has both a QR code generator and a QR code reader

Procedures

Before beginning this lesson, students must have prior knowledge about the elements of a story—characters, plots, setting, themes, and so on. Before the students begin to produce their book trailer, the teacher and/or librarian will show several examples of trailers to discuss the elements that make a good trailer. The librarian will demonstrate how to create a video using each site and provide a handout to guide the students (see appendix for handouts). The librarian will also teach students how to search for images and videos and cite the sources.

After reading a book, students will complete the stage one lesson plan to create a storyboard/script for a 30-second book trailer and then use One True Media or Animoto to produce the book trailer. The storyboard/script will include these elements:

1. Book title and author name

2. A statement that the book is available to check out in the library

3. At least two statements that can be used to hook a reader

The student will be given a choice of using either One True Media (http://www.onetruemedia.com) or Animoto (http://animoto.com) to create his or her book trailer. They are both free video tools that can be used to create videos from uploaded images, short videos, and short text. Animoto allows 55 characters per text slide, and One True Media allows 80 characters per text slide. Larger text can be entered on a PowerPoint slide and saved as an image file to upload to the sites. The videos can be created with Creative Commons pictures and videos from the Internet (with proper credit given), or students can use their own pictures and videos. Both sites provide various free effects such animations, transitions, and music. While Animoto randomizes the effects, One True Media allows users complete control of the editing process. One True Media users are able to choose both the montage style and all of the movements within that montage. Both sites allow the user to upload directly to YouTube or email the finished video with one click of a button. The book trailer must state that the book is available in the library (for example "Now available at a library near you").

The book trailer can be shown in classrooms or to the entire school through the morning announcements. The book trailers can be set to run continuously on a television or computer in the library for patrons to use to identify books they want to check out. The book trailers can be linked on the library's online card catalog system, linked on the school website, or shown continuously through a digital picture frame displayed in a prominent place for patrons to view. A rubric given before the project is started will keep students on track and allow students to understand how they will be graded (see rubric at the end of the lesson plan).

Extension: QR Codes

Once the students have created their book trailers, a QR code can be generated and glued to the inside cover of the book. By scanning these codes with their

smartphone, patrons could view the book trailer to decide if they want to check out the book. See this example trailer created using One True Media, for the book *Dirty Little Secret* by C. J. Omololu (http://www.youtube.com/watch?v = hWVjgImPum8):

Free websites can be used to generate a QR code within seconds. This QR code was created by Quikqr (http://quikqr.com), a site that has both a free QR code generator and a free QR code reader. A QR code reader app must be installed on smartphones in order to actually scan the bar code. The short, simple directions for generating a QR code using Quikqr are as follows:

1. Go to Quikqr at http://quikqr.com.

2. Enter a URL or text that you want the QR code to direct users to.

3. Hit the "Generate Code" button.

Once the code is generated, it can be saved by clicking the "Save QR Code as a PNG image" button or by entering your email address to have it sent directly to you. Once the code is saved, it can be printed and displayed anywhere—on books, on bulletin boards, on websites, and so forth.

TABLE 3.6   Thirty-Second Book Trailer Rubric

Elements	Exemplary 3	Satisfactory but lacking in some areas 2	Needs improvement 1	Score
Text slides	Text slides included meet or exceed the minimum requirement of five text slides. One text slide should include the book title and author name, one text slide should indicate that the book is available for check out in the library, a citation slide should provide credits for any pictures used, and the remaining two or more text slides should be used to hook the reader.	Missing one or two of the minimum requirement of five text slides. Required text slides include: one text slide should include the book title and author name, one text slide should indicate that the book is available for check out in the library, a citation slide should provide credits for any pictures used, and the remaining two text slides should be used to hook the reader.	Missing three or more of the minimum requirement of five text slides. Required text slides include: one text slide should include the book title and author name, one text slide should indicate that the book is available for check out in the library, a citation slide should provide credits for any pictures used, and the remaining two text slides should be used to hook the reader.	
Pictures	Pictures included meet or exceed the minimum requirement of four pictures. Pictures should represent a significant element from the book such as the main character(s), outline of the major story plot, identification of the setting and or time period of the story, and identification of the major themes of the story. Pictures follow the text slides they represent.	Missing one or two of the required four pictures. Pictures should represent a significant element from the book such as the main character(s), outline of the major story plot, identification of the setting and or time period of the story, and identification of the major themes of the story. Pictures follow the text slides they represent.	Missing the required four pictures or pictures seem random, thus making it hard to understand how they represent the book.	

(continued)

TABLE 3.6   **Thirty-Second Book Trailer Rubric**   *(continued)*

Elements	Exemplary 3	Satisfactory but lacking in some areas 2	Needs improvement 1	Score
Technical Production	Video editing software was used to create a professional-looking video book trailer. Music chosen is appropriate and not distracting. Special effects and transitions are smooth and not distracting. Video length adheres to the 30-second time limit to keep the audience interested and engaged.	Video editing software was used to create but most features of the software were not used. Music chosen is appropriate and not distracting. Special effects and transitions are smooth and not distracting. Video length is 5 to 10 seconds too short.	No video editing software was used to produce the book trailer so video consists of recorded video only with no additional pictures, effects, transitions, or text. Music chosen is inappropriate, distracting, or makes any narration inaudible. Video length is less than 15 seconds.	
Overall construction	Creativity and originality enhance the viewing experience. Book trailer engages the audience in an entertaining way. Able to hook a reader to check out the book.	Shows some creativity and originality but needs improvement to draw the viewer in. Book trailer does not engage or entertain the audience as much as it could.	Lacks creativity and originality, which makes the book trailer boring or not engaging. Does not encourage other people to read the book.	

Total score (out of 12)

> **Suggestions for Videos You Can Create and Post to a Media Sharing Website, Such as a YouTube Channel**
>
> • Post a virtual tour of your library.
>
> • Post advertisements to encourage library use.
>
> • Post steps that walk patrons through different tasks that they might need help from a librarian to accomplish, such as the steps of the research process, how to search the Internet for information, how to check out a book, how to use databases, how to cite sources, and so forth.

Stage Three: Two-Minute Book Trailer Lesson Plan

Overview

The stage two lesson can become a stage three lesson by creating a longer two-minute storyboard/script and book trailer. A stage three lesson would require students to use the computer to type text, find images, create a two-minute book trailer, and upload their video to YouTube for everyone to view.

Information and Technology Literacy Standards

NETS5.a Students advocate and practice safe, legal, and responsible use of information and technology.

NETS5.b Students exhibit a positive attitude toward using technology that supports collaboration, learning, and productivity.

NETS5.c Students demonstrate personal responsibility for lifelong learning.

NETS5.d Students exhibit leadership for digital citizenship.

Common Core State Standards

CC.5–8.L.3 Students use knowledge of language and its conventions when writing, speaking, reading, or listening.

CC.7.L.3.a Students choose language that expresses ideas precisely and concisely, recognizing and eliminating wordiness and redundancy.

CC.9–12.L.3 Students apply knowledge of language to understand how language functions in different contexts, to make effective choices for meaning or style, and to comprehend more fully when reading or listening.

CC.6.S.L.5 Students include multimedia components (e.g., graphics, image, music, sound) and visual displays in presentations to clarify information.

CC.7.S.L.5 Students include multimedia components and visual displays in presentations to clarify claims and findings and emphasize salient points.

CC.8.S.L.5 Students include multimedia components and visual displays into presentations to clarify information, strengthen claims and evidence, and add interest.

CC.9–12.S.L.5 Students make strategic use of digital media (e.g., textual, graphical, audio, visual, and interactive elements) in presentations to enhance understanding of findings, reasoning, and evidence and to add interest.

CC.5.R.L.2 Students determine a theme of a story, drama, or poem from details in the text, including how characters in a story or drama respond to challenges or how the speaker in a poem reflects upon a topic; summarize the text.

CC.6.R.L.2 Students determine a theme or central idea of a text and how it is conveyed through particular details; provide a summary of the text distinct from personal opinions or judgments.

CC.7.R.L.2 Students determine a theme or central idea of a text and analyze its development over the course of the text; provide an objective summary of the text.

CC.8.R.L.2 Students determine a theme or central idea of a text and analyze its development over the course of the text, including its relationship to the characters, setting, and plot; provide an objective summary of the text.

CC.9–10.R.L.2 Students determine a theme or central idea of a text and analyze in detail its development over the course of the text, including how it emerges and is shaped and refined by specific details; provide an objective summary of the text.

CC.11–12.R.L.2 Determine two or more themes or central ideas of a text and analyze their development over the course of the text, including how they interact and build on one another to produce a complex account; provide an objective summary of the text.

Additional Resources Worth Checking Out

Book Trailers for All (http://booktrailersforall.com) is a website dedicated to resources for educators and students to assist with creating, downloading, and sharing book trailers. Website includes ready-to-use handouts, examples of book trailers, and training opportunities.

The Happy Scientist (http://www.thehappyscientist.com), created by Robert Krampf, has daily science news and "experiment of the week" videos. More than 19,000 people a day view his daily science photo quiz on Facebook.

The Khan Academy (http://www.khanacademy.org), created by Salman Khan, has thousands of 10- to 20-minute video lectures on numerous topics such as economics, trigonometry, history, and so on. The videos explain complex subjects in simple language with drawings and diagrams to illustrate concepts.

NurdRage's (http://www.youtube.com/user/nurdrage?blend = 1&ob = 4) YouTube channel consists of over 100 videos of science experiments, from growing silver metal crystals to levitating pencil graphite with magnets. The vloggers that produce the videos consist of a group of anonymous Canadian chemistry and biology researchers. While the scientists never show their faces, they work in a full lab setting and include a description of both the scientific processes and safety hazards in each experiment.

Watch Know Learn (http://www.watchknow.org) contains thousands of short educational videos, and other media, explaining topics taught in school.

YouTube offers numerous customizable resources for your library. It is a good idea to create a YouTube channel for your library and customize it to fit your needs. On your library channel you can subscribe to the best channels. The channels you subscribe to will be those that you recommend to your students, teachers, and patrons. They can go directly to your channel and then just go to your recommended sites through your subscriptions section. That way they do not waste time searching through the other unrelated or worthless videos. With millions of YouTube channels out there, who really has time to search for the best-quality videos? Here is a compiled list of YouTube channels to consider subscribing to (and a brief description if the title does not clearly indicate what should be found on the channel):

American Library Association http://www.youtube.com/user/AmLibraryAssociation

---

Additional Resources Worth Checking Out

American Museum of Natural History http://www.youtube.com/user/AMNHorg

American Poet Academy http://www.youtube.com/user/poetsacademy

Associated Press http://www.youtube.com/user/AssociatedPress

Book TV http://www.youtube.com/user/BookTV (Here you can see the latest in nonfiction books: history, biography, politics, current events, the media, and more. Watch author interviews, readings, parties, panels, and book fairs and festivals from across the country.)

CBS News http://www.youtube.com/user/CBSNewsOnline

Centers for Disease Control and Prevention (CDC) http://www.youtube.com/user/CDCStreamingHealth

Discovery Networks http://www.youtube.com/user/DiscoveryNetworks (Provides stories and experiences from the world of science, natural history, anthropology, survival, geography, and engineering.)

FDR Library and Museum http://www.youtube.com/user/FDRLibrary (The mission of the Franklin D. Roosevelt Presidential Library and Museum is to foster research and education on the life and times of Franklin and Eleanor Roosevelt and their continuing impact on contemporary life. The site also has videos on the Great Depression and World War II.)

Hachette Book Group http://www.youtube.com/user/HachetteBookGroup

HarperTeen http://www.youtube.com/user/harperteen

Library of Congress http://www.youtube.com/user/LibraryOfCongress

Little Brown Books http://www.youtube.com/user/LittleBrownBooks

National Aeronautics and Space Administration (NASA) http://www.youtube.com/user/NASAtelevision

National Geographic http://www.youtube.com/user/NationalGeographic

National Oceanic and Atmospheric Administration (NOAA) http://www.youtube.com/user/oceanexplorergov

New York Times http://www.youtube.com/user/TheNewYorkTimes

Resources Needed

Library or classroom book

A two-minute storyboard/script from a modified stage one lesson plan

Computers with Internet access

Networking Media Used

YouTube (http://www.youtube.com), TeacherTube (http://teachertube.com), and Wikimedia Commons (http://commons.wikimedia.org) to show book and movie trailers

Creative Commons (http://search.creativecommons.org) to find images

JayCut (http://jaycut.com) to produce the book trailer

Animoto for Education (http://animoto.com/education) to produce the book trailer

Quikqr (http://quikqr.com) is a free website that has both a QR code generator and a QR code reader

Procedures

After reading a book, students will write a script for a two-minute book trailer and then use Animoto educational version or JayCut to produce the book trailer. The script will include these elements:

1. Book title and author name

2. A statement that the book is available to check out in the library

3. A book summary and a statement that can be used to hook a reader

4. Description of pictures that will follow text

Before beginning this lesson, students must have prior knowledge about the elements of a story—characters, plots, setting, themes, and so on. Before the students begin to produce their book trailer, the teacher and/or librarian will show several examples of trailers to discuss the elements that make a good trailer. The librarian will demonstrate how to create a video using each site and provide a handout to guide the students (see appendix for handouts). The librarian will also teach students how to search for images and videos and cite the sources. The book trailer must state that the book is available in the library (for example "This book is not to be missed and is now available at a library near you").

Students will then convert that script into a two-minute book trailer to advertise that library book. The student will be given a choice of using either JayCut (http://jaycut.com) or Animoto for Education (http://animoto.com/education) to create their book trailer. Animoto allows educators and students to sign up for free educational subscriptions that allow videos up to 10 minutes while the regular free version only allows videos up to 30 seconds. JayCut is another free resource that allows video creations up to 10 minutes. They are both video tools in which users create videos from uploaded images, short videos, and short text. Animoto allows 55 characters per text slide and JayCut allows unlimited characters per text slide, but users should limit text to allow viewers to read all text on the screen. Longer text can be entered on a PowerPoint slide and saved as an image file to upload to the sites. The videos can be created with still pictures and videos from the Internet (with proper credit given), or students can use their own pictures and videos. Both sites are free but offer added features if you pay minimal fees. Both sites allow the user to upload directly to YouTube with one click of a button.

The book trailer can be shown in classrooms or to the entire school through the morning announcements. The students must upload their video to YouTube in order to be graded. The book trailers can be set to run continuously on a television or computer in the library for patrons to use to identify books they want to check out. The book trailers can be linked on the library's on-line card catalog system, linked on the school website, or shown continuously through a digital picture frame displayed in a prominent place for patrons to view. A rubric given before the project is started will keep students on track and allow students to understand how they will be graded (see rubric at the end of the lesson plan).

> ### Additional Resources Worth Checking Out
>
> **NOVA** http://www.youtube.com/user/NOVAonline (NOVA is the most watched science television series in the world and the most watched documentary series on PBS.)
>
> **PBS** http://www.youtube.com/user/PBS
>
> **Penguin Young Readers Books** http://www.youtube.com/user/PenguinYoungReaders
>
> **Poetry Out Loud** http://www.youtube.com/watch?v = K_6LaP1A3OA
>
> **School Library Journal** http://www.youtube.com/user/SchoolLibJournal
>
> **Simon & Schuster Books** http://www.youtube.com/user/SimonSchusterVideos
>
> **Smithsonian Air and Space Museum** http://www.youtube.com/user/airandspace
>
> **Smithsonian American History Museum** http://www.youtube.com/user/SmithsonianAmHistory
>
> **Smithsonian Channel** http://www.youtube.com/user/smithsonianchannel
>
> **Smithsonian Libraries** http://www.youtube.com/user/SmithsonianLibraries (This video channel features content produced by the Smithsonian Institution Libraries.)
>
> **U.S. Food and Drug Administration (FDA)** http://www.youtube.com/user/USFoodandDrugAdmin
>
> **U.S. Government** http://www.youtube.com/user/USGovernment
>
> **Wall Street Journal** http://www.youtube.com/user/WSJDigitalNetwork

Extension: QR Codes

Once the students have created their book trailers, a QR code can be generated and glued to the inside cover of the book. By scanning these codes with their smartphone, patrons could view the book trailer to decide if they want to check out the book. See this example trailer created using Animoto for Education, for the book *Ship Breaker* by Paolo Bacigalupi (http://www.youtube.com/user/gamediacenter#p/u/6/kXa2ary4rSo):

Free websites can be used to generate a QR code within seconds. This QR code was created by Quikqr (http://quikqr.com), a site that has both a free QR code generator and a free QR code reader. A QR code reader app must be installed on smartphones in order to actually scan the bar code. The short, simple directions for generating a QR code using Quikqr are as follows:

1. Go to Quikqr at http://quikqr.com.

2. Enter a URL or text that you want the QR code to direct users to.

3. Hit the "Generate Code" button.

Once the code is generated, it can be saved by clicking the "Save QR Code as a PNG image" button or by entering your email address to have it sent directly to you. Once the code is saved, it can be printed and displayed anywhere—on books, on bulletin boards, on websites, and so forth.

TABLE 3.7　Two-Minute YouTube Book Trailer Rubric

Elements	Exemplary 3	Satisfactory but lacking in some areas 2	Needs improvement 1	Score
Book summary	Book trailer clearly and accurately summarizes the book with sufficient detail. The book trailer has a minimum of all four of these elements: identification of the main character(s), outline of the major story plot, identification of the setting and or time period of the story, and identification of the major themes of the story. All details of the book should be provided without giving the climax or ending away.	Summary information is not completely accurate, not clearly presented, or presented in a way that spoils part of the story for a reader by giving away too many details. Information is missing one or two of these elements: identification of the main character(s), outline of the major story plot, identification of the setting and or time period of the story, and identification of the major themes of the story.	Summary information is incomplete, off topic, inaccurate, or presented in a way that spoils part of the story for a reader by giving away too many details. Information is missing three or four of these elements: identification of the main character(s), outline of the major story plot, identification of the setting and or time period of the story, and identification of the major themes of the story.	
Organization	Book title and author are clearly identified. Clear, accurate information is presented. Thoughts are organized and flow smoothly. Book trailer clearly states that the book can be checked out from the library. All pictures,	Book title is clearly identified but author is not. Some basic information is not accurate or not clearly presented. Thoughts are organized. The book trailer encourages the viewer to get the book but does not state that it is available	Book title and author are not clearly identified. Basic information is incomplete, off topic, or inaccurate. Little organization. Book trailer never indicates that the book can be checked out from the library. No credit slide at the end.	

TABLE 3.7 **Two-Minute YouTube Book Trailer Rubric** (*continued*)

Elements	Exemplary 3	Satisfactory but lacking in some areas 2	Needs improvement 1	Score
Organization	videos, and other text sources are cited properly in MLA format on a credit slide at the end.	in the library. All pictures, videos, and other text sources are cited on a credit slide at the end but there are some minor errors in the MLA format.		
Pictures	Pictures included meet or exceed the minimum requirement of 10 pictures. Required pictures include one of the book jacket, one of the author, and the remaining eight pictures should represent significant elements from the book such as the main character(s), outline of the major story plot, identification of the setting and or time period of the story, and identification of the major themes of the story.	Missing from one to four of the required pictures. Required pictures include one of the book jacket, one of the author, and the remaining eight pictures should represent significant elements from the book such as the main character(s), outline of the major story plot, identification of the setting and or time period of the story, and identification of the major themes of the story.	Missing five or more of the required pictures. Required pictures include one of the book jacket, one of the author, and the remaining eight pictures should represent significant elements from the book such as the main character(s), outline of the major story plot, identification of the setting and or time period of the story, and identification of the major themes of the story.	
Technical production	Video editing software was used to create a professional-looking video book trailer. Music chosen is appropriate and not distracting. Special effects and transitions are smooth and not distracting. Video length adheres to the two-minute time limit to keep the audience interested and engaged. Book trailer was uploaded to YouTube and marked as public.	Video editing software was used to create but most features of the software were not used. Music chosen is appropriate and not distracting. Special effects and transitions are smooth and not distracting. Video length is 10 to 30 seconds too short or too long. Book trailer was uploaded to YouTube and marked as private or unlisted.	No video editing software was used to produce the book trailer so video consists of recorded video only with no additional pictures, effects, transitions, or text. Music chosen is inappropriate, distracting, or makes any narration inaudible. Video length is less than 45 seconds or more than two minutes and 30 seconds. Book trailer was not uploaded to YouTube.	
Overall construction	Creativity and originality enhance the viewing experience of the book trailer. The book trailer engages the audience in an entertaining way. Able to hook a reader to check out the book.	The book trailer shows some creativity and originality but could be improved. Book trailer does not engage or entertain the audience as much as it could.	The book trailer lacks creativity and originality, which makes the trailer boring or not engaging. Does not encourage other people to read the book.	

Total score (out of 15)

Lesson Plans Adapted for Other Subjects

Use social studies learning standards to assign students a project to create videos to illustrate a current event or event in history.

Use science learning standards to assign students a project to create videos depicting a new concept from the textbook. It can be adapted to any textbook students are reading and provides a quick, spontaneous activity that helps students engage in what they are reading.

Use math learning standards to assign students a project to create videos to depict a scene or an event using math story problems. It can be adapted to any math concepts to help students engage in what they are learning.

4

Microblogs and Wikis in the Classroom

Terms to Know

Avatar—A computer-generated representation of a character. An avatar can be two- or three-dimensional and is animated.

Blog—A shortened form of the words *Web log*. A blog is a journal, diary, or other collection of writing and information that is usually displayed in reverse chronological order with the newest posts at the top. A typical blog combines text, images, links, and other media related to its topic.

Blogger—Someone who writes a blog.

Blogging—Process of writing a blog.

Blogosphere—Term used to describe the world of blogs, including the blogs themselves, the space where bloggers interact, the jargon associated with blogs, and the culture surrounding blogs. The term also is used to refer to the space where blogs are found—the Internet.

Educational networking—Term used to describe the use of social networking technologies and ideas for educational purposes.

Follower—Refer to someone that subscribes to a blog or microblog in order to keep up with all the latest blog and microblog posts for their selected sites.

Hashtag—Used in Twitter and other microblogging services to group posts about a specific topic together to make searching for that topic easy. A hashtag consists of the hash symbol (#) followed by words or phrases.

Microblog—A short, concise journal, diary, or other collection of writing and information that is usually displayed in reverse chronological order with the newest posts at the top. The short exchange of information encourages more interaction between the blogger and followers.

Multimedia—Mixing printed words, video, sound, and pictures in one place, such as videos that appear in the middle of webpages.

Podcast—An audio recording available online. The word *podcasting* is a combination of the words *iPod* and *broadcasting*.

Retweet—Sending out a tweet on Twitter that is the exact posting of someone else's tweet with their username attached to ensure they are given credit for the original tweet. A high rate of retweets can indicate a high success rate with getting information out using Twitter because the more times information is retweeted, the more people it reaches.

Why Use Microblogging and Wiki Sites?

We are in the middle of a communication revolution as people now share intimate details of their life as fast as they can type. In this mobile, Internet-engrossed world, everyone can have their voice heard in an instant with little or no technical skills. Wikis, blogs, and microblogs are used by millions of people every day to discuss their lives and the news of the day. The dated one-way flow of information from book or website to patron just does not work for patrons anymore; they need to interact with their information. Not only do patrons need to interact with the librarians who serve them, but students need to interact with their teachers and their classmates for authentic learning experiences.

Students want to be heard, and they want their work to be seen. Publishing work for an authentic audience empowers students. Having an authentic audience encourages students to do their best work because when writing becomes public, it ceases to be just another assignment they hand in to the teacher. In this Internet age, anyone can be a published author in an instant. There are so many free and easy publishing methods online that it is hard to choose the right one—wiki, blog, or microblog. Put simply, blogs are one-to-many communications, wikis are many-to-many communications, and microblogs are short one-to-many communications that encourage replies and feedback to posts. All of these publishing options can have these effects: improve student writing through regular practice; decrease inhibition during class discussion by allowing everyone a chance to have their voice heard; encourage self-editing by requiring students to edit their posts before publishing; and allow practice of standards-based writing strategies, such as summarizing.

The best dialogues occur when students interact with one another—asking each other probing and thought-provoking questions, complementing and commenting on one another's thoughts, and adding to the discussion with new information. In a confined classroom with limited time, it is almost impossible to give every student in a class an opportunity to speak. Some students are shy and inhibited from participating in class discussions, while other students constantly dominate the classroom discussions. If used effectively, online discussion minimizes these challenges by providing every student an opportunity to have his or her voice heard.

Text messaging and networking sites are common ways for students to communicate on a daily basis. So they are already familiar and comfortable with these forms of communication. Reading and writing texts online are basic skills that students need to be literate citizens in the 21st century. Wikis and microblogging sites can allow students to interact in a two-way conversation online, anytime, anywhere. Note that I am focusing on microblog sites here and not blog sites because

Venn Diagram Showing the Similarities and Differences Between Microblogs and Wikis

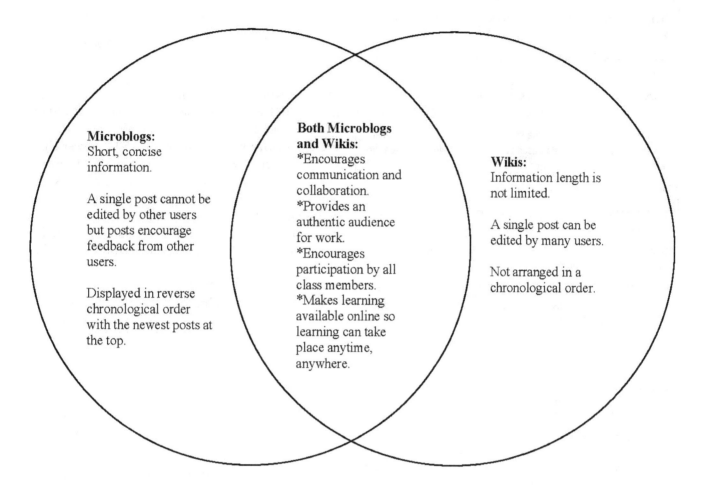

Microblogs:
Short, concise information.

A single post cannot be edited by other users but posts encourage feedback from other users.

Displayed in reverse chronological order with the newest posts at the top.

Both Microblogs and Wikis:
*Encourages communication and collaboration.
*Provides an authentic audience for work.
*Encourages participation by all class members.
*Makes learning available online so learning can take place anytime, anywhere.

Wikis:
Information length is not limited.

A single post can be edited by many users.

Not arranged in a chronological order.

blog sites are synonymous with writers pushing out content, whereas microblog services encourage feedback and two-way communication. Blogs are considered a social media and are wonderful tools to use in classrooms to give students authentic audiences instead of being limited to just one teacher. However, one of the main focuses of this book is to increase interaction and engagement, and microblogging is a better means than blogging to create dialogue with students. Another good point about microblogging sites is that they force students to be concise and to the point, which helps meet many Common Core State Standards that deal with summarizing skills. Using wikis and microblog sites is effective at increasing classroom dialogue, because they enable *all* students to contribute during lessons without feeling pressured. Even the students who are the most reluctant to talk in class will be able to express their thoughts on a wiki or microblog.

Microblogging and Wiki Lesson Plans

The following lesson plans incorporate microblogging and wiki sites such as Twitter and PBworks to share information, pictures, and audio recordings. These lessons can replicate face-to-face literature circles but in a way in which everyone must participate and no one person can monopolize the discussion. The three stages of lesson plans allow anyone to incorporate the idea of microblogging and wiki networking sites into their classroom regardless of technology restrictions.

Stage One: Book Summary on Paper Lesson Plan

Overview

Students will check out a library book on their reading level or have a book assigned for classroom reading. After reading a chapter or section in the book, students will summarize what happened in 150 or fewer characters. Students will write these summaries from the perspective of one of the characters in the book. At the end of the book, the summaries will be placed together and should tell the basic story of the whole book. Stage one users have limited access to technology or the Internet, so technology is usually utilized by the teacher for demonstration and display purposes. To overcome these technology obstacles, this particular lesson requires the teacher or librarian to use the technology for production and the students to only view the technology through a teacher presentation.

Common Core State Standards

CC.5–8.L.3 Students use knowledge of language and its conventions when writing, speaking, reading, or listening.

CC.7.L.3.a Students choose language that expresses ideas precisely and concisely, recognizing and eliminating wordiness and redundancy.

CC.9–12.L.3 Students apply knowledge of language to understand how language functions in different contexts, to make effective choices for meaning or style, and to comprehend more fully when reading or listening.

CC.5.R.L.2 Students determine a theme of a story, drama, or poem from details in the text, including how characters in a story or drama respond to challenges or how the speaker in a poem reflects upon a topic; summarize the text.

CC.6.R.L.2 Students determine a theme or central idea of a text and how it is conveyed through particular details; provide a summary of the text distinct from personal opinions or judgments.

CC.7.R.L.2 Students determine a theme or central idea of a text and analyze its development over the course of the text; provide an objective summary of the text.

CC.8.R.L.2 Students determine a theme or central idea of a text and analyze its development over the course of the text, including its relationship to the characters, setting, and plot; provide an objective summary of the text.

Chapter Summary Handout

Your Name: _____

Book Title: _____

Book Author: _____

Chapter or Page Numbers: _____

Character Name: _____

_____ **writes**

_____
_____
_____
_____
_____
_____
_____
_____
_____
_____
_____
_____
_____
_____

| SHARE |

Note: Punctuation and spaces between words count as characters.

CC.9–10.R.L.2 Students determine a theme or central idea of a text and analyze in detail its development over the course of the text, including how it emerges and is shaped and refined by specific details; provide an objective summary of the text.

CC.11–12.R.L.2 Determine two or more themes or central ideas of a text and analyze their development over the course of the text, including how they interact and build on one another to produce a complex account; provide an objective summary of the text.

Resources Needed

Library or classroom book

Chapter Summary Handout and pens/pencils

Networking Sites to Know

Twitter (http://twitter.com) is a social networking and microblogging service that enables its users to send and read messages up to 140 characters long (known as tweets).

Wikipedia (http://wikipedia.org) is a combination of the words *wiki* and *encyclopedia*. The site is a free online encyclopedia that allows contributors to collaboratively create the entries.

Wikispaces for Teachers (http://www.wikispaces.com/content/for/teachers) is a website that allows users to set up a free wiki workspace that can be private or public.

YouTube (http://www.youtube.com) is a website to watch and share originally created videos.

Twitter (http://twitter.com) or other site such as Historical Tweets (http://historicaltweets.com) and Such Tweet Sorrow (http://www.suchtweetsorrow.com) to show students examples of tweets so they know what they are expected to do

Videos on YouTube (http://www.youtube.com) or Common Craft (http://www.commoncraft.com) to view an introduction to the lesson

Procedures

Students will chose a library book to read on their reading level (or this lesson can be used for a required classroom reading assignment). This lesson requires the teacher and librarian to introduce the Twitter website to the students and work with the students to practice summarizing text in a very concise way. A discussion should take place to see how familiar students are with Twitter. The librarian should explain that Twitter is a microblogging service and show appropriate examples from the Twitter site or another site that can serve as an accurate model for their summaries.

To begin the lesson, the Common Craft website offers a good introduction to what Twitter is in the video *Twitter in Plain English* (http://commoncraft.com/twitter). Two sites, other than Twitter, that could be used to show example tweets include the website Historical Tweets (http://historicaltweets.com) and Such Tweet Sorrow (http://www.suchtweetsorrow.com). Historical Tweets is an entertaining site that allows contributors to create tweets from famous people in history. Not all entries are appropriate, so it is best to search the site in advance for good examples and bookmark or copy them to share with students. There are examples of appropriate Historical Tweets on the author's blog. Some examples of people with Historical Tweets include Abraham Lincoln, Neil Armstrong, Harriet Tubman, Anne Frank, and John Hancock. Students would have to understand the famous person's significance in history or know general details about the person to understand the humor of these tweets.

Such Tweet Sorrow is Shakespeare's famous play, *Romeo and Juliet*, performed as tweets from the characters. Students who follow the tweet will be able to read tweets from each character in the story (with each post being 140 characters or fewer, of course) to get the whole story. The Royal Shakespeare Company (RSC) and Mudlark, a mobile entertainment producer, have teamed up to create the site. Of course, students will not be able to read the tweets and avoid Shakespeare's writing all together, but students will be able to engage in active discussions comparing the tweets to the texts for a fuller learning experience.

The teacher and librarian will need to practice reading text as a whole class and summarizing that passage in a succinct way that adheres to the 150-character maximum. Students will need to develop the skills necessary to pick out important points from text and summarize those important points in order to complete this assignment. Students will need to understand

---

Other Websites Used in the Lessons

Book Nut (http://www.thebooknut.com) is a blog that features book reviews. The blogger reviews some adult fiction, but the bulk of her posts are for children and young adults. She includes age ranges on each book review she posts.

Children's Books Wiki (http://childrensbooks.wikia.com/wiki/Children%27s_Books_Wiki) is a wiki that allows anyone to contribute to the site by adding reviews, editing reviews, adding additional information to reviews, or commenting on the reviews. Each book has a description, readers' reviews, guidance on content, recommended reading age, and links to other similar books. Books reviewed on the site include children's through young adult books.

Guys Lit Wire (http://guyslitwire.blogspot.com) is a blog featuring books that are of interest to teenage boys and is written by over 20 contributors from various demographics and backgrounds including a teacher, a librarian, a book seller, a journalist, and a student.

Historical Tweets (http://historicaltweets.com) is an entertaining site that allows contributors to create tweets from famous people in history. Some examples of people found on the site include Abraham Lincoln, Neil Armstrong, Harriet Tubman, Anne Frank, and John Hancock.

TABLE 4.1   Book Summary on Paper Rubric

Elements	Exemplary 3	Satisfactory but lacking in some areas 2	Needs improvement 1	Score
Summary content	Clear, accurate summary of the book is presented.	Some information is partially inaccurate or not directly related to the summary of the story.	Information is incomplete, off topic, or inaccurate.	
Perspective	All summaries are first person from the perspective of the character. Perspective is accurate for the chosen character.	Most summaries are first person from the perspective of the character. Perspective is somewhat accurate for the chosen character.	Summaries are not first person from the perspective of the character. Perspective is not accurate for the chosen character.	
Creativity	Summaries are original and creative.	Summaries are original but lack some creativity.	Summaries are not original (direct quotes from book) and lack creativity.	
Mechanics	Handwriting is legible. No errors in spelling, grammar, capitalization, or punctuation.	Handwriting may be difficult to read in places. Two or less errors in spelling, grammar, capitalization, or punctuation.	Handwriting is illegible. Three or more errors in spelling, grammar, capitalization, or punctuation.	
Frequency	Exceeds the number of summaries required by having at least one summary per chapter or assigned section.	Meets the minimum number of original summaries by having only one summary per chapter or assigned section.	Does not meet the minimum number of original summaries by having less than one summary per chapter or assigned section.	

Total score (out of 15)

the following specifics: writing must be precise and clear; long words should be avoided; information should be implied rather than stated; and declarative sentences and questions are effective ways to communicate. Students will complete their summaries on the Chapter Summary Handout to ensure that fewer than 150 characters are used. A rubric given before the project is started will keep students on track and allow students to understand how they will be graded (see the rubric at the end of this lesson plan).

Stage Two: Book Summary Lesson Plan

Overview

The stage one lesson can easily be carried into a stage two lesson plan by having students complete the stage one lesson on a private classroom wiki. After reading a chapter or section in a book, students will summarize what happened in 150 or fewer characters. Students will write these summaries from the perspective of one of the characters in the book. At the end of the book, the summaries will be placed together and should tell the basic story of the whole book. A stage

Other Websites Used in the Lessons

In Plain English Videos (http://www.commoncraft.com) are simple videos explaining different technology terms in language that anyone can understand. These videos are created by Common Craft LLC.

Quikqr (http://quikqr.com) is a free website that has both a QR code generator and a QR code reader.

Such Tweet Sorrow (http://www.suchtweetsorrow.com) is Shakespeare's famous play, *Romeo and Juliet,* performed as tweets from the characters. Students who follow the tweet will be able to read tweets from each character in the story (with each post being 140 characters or less, of course) to get the whole story.

Tagxedo (http://www.tagxedo.com) is a free website that generates a visual word cloud of text that a user provides. The word cloud image gives greater prominence to words that appear more frequently in the source text to allow a viewer to see the dominant concepts of the text easily. Users can manipulate the fonts, layouts, and color schemes and can choose a customized shape for the word clouds.

Vocaroo (http://vocaroo.com) is a free online service that allows users to create audio recordings without the need to install any software. All you need to provide is a microphone. The audio recording can be embed into wikis, blogs, and websites. The site requires very little technical skill and makes embedding the audio very simple.

Voki (http://www.voki.com) is a service that allows users to create animated audio avatars. The online service allows users to create audio recordings without the need to install any software. All you need to provide is a microphone. The avatar can be embed into wikis, blogs, and websites. The site requires very little technical skill and makes embedding the avatar very simple.

Wiki Summaries (http://www.wikisummaries.org) is a wiki similar to Wikipedia that allows contributors to submit book summaries. Anyone can contribute by adding summaries, editing summaries, adding additional information to summaries, or commenting on the summary.

Wordle (http://www.wordle.net) is a free website that generates a visual word cloud of text that a user provides. The word clouds give greater prominence to words that appear more frequently in the source text to allow a viewer to see the dominant concepts of the text easily. Users can manipulate the fonts, layouts, and color schemes of the word clouds.

---

two lesson would require students to use the computer to type their summaries in the provided template and then post that document to a secure wiki. This educational wiki site is a stage two lesson because all posts made by students can only be viewed by the teacher and other members of the class.

Information and Technology Literacy Standards

NETS5.a Students advocate and practice safe, legal, and responsible use of information and technology.

NETS5.b Students exhibit a positive attitude toward using technology that supports collaboration, learning, and productivity.

NETS5.c Students demonstrate personal responsibility for lifelong learning.

NETS5.d Students exhibit leadership for digital citizenship.

Common Core State Standards

CC.5–8.L.3 Students use knowledge of language and its conventions when writing, speaking, reading, or listening.

CC.7.L.3.a Students choose language that expresses ideas precisely and concisely, recognizing and eliminating wordiness and redundancy.

CC.9–12.L.3 Students apply knowledge of language to understand how language functions in different contexts, to make effective choices for meaning or style, and to comprehend more fully when reading or listening.

CC.5.R.L.2 Students determine a theme of a story, drama, or poem from details in the text, including how characters in a story or drama respond to challenges or how the speaker in a poem reflects upon a topic; summarize the text.

CC.6.R.L.2 Students determine a theme or central idea of a text and how it is conveyed through particular details; provide a summary of the text distinct from personal opinions or judgments.

CC.7.R.L.2 Students determine a theme or central idea of a text and analyze its development over the course of the text; provide an objective summary of the text.

CC.8.R.L.2 Students determine a theme or central idea of a text and analyze its development over the course of the text, including its relationship to the characters, setting, and plot; provide an objective summary of the text.

CC.9–10.R.L.2 Students determine a theme or central idea of a text and analyze in detail its development over the course of the text, including how it

emerges and is shaped and refined by specific details; provide an objective summary of the text.

CC.11–12.R.L.2 Determine two or more themes or central ideas of a text and analyze their development over the course of the text, including how they interact and build on one another to produce a complex account; provide an objective summary of the text.

Resources Needed

Library or classroom book

Chapter Summary Handout to edit on the computer

Computers with Internet access

Networking Media Used

PBworks (http://pbworks.com) or Wikispaces for Teachers (http://www.wikispaces.com/content/for/teachers) to post tweets to a private site that can only be viewed and edited by the teacher and students in the class

Twitter (http://twitter.com) or other site such as Historical Tweets (http://historicaltweets.com) and Such Tweet Sorrow (http://www.suchtweetsorrow.com) to show students examples of tweets so they know what they are expected to do

Guys Lit Wire (http://guyslitwire.blogspot.com), Book Nut (http://www.thebooknut.com), and Wiki Summaries (http://www.wikisummaries.org) to show students examples of blogs and wikis as well as book reviews and book summaries

Videos on YouTube (http://www.youtube.com) or Common Craft (http://www.commoncraft.com) to view an introduction to the lesson

Procedures

Students will chose a library book to read on their reading level (or this lesson can be used for a required classroom reading assignment). This lesson requires the teacher and librarian to introduce the Twitter website to the students and work with the students to practice summarizing text in a very concise way. A discussion should take place to see how familiar students are with Twitter. The librarian should explain that Twitter is a microblogging service and show appropriate examples from the Twitter site or another site that can serve as an accurate model for their summaries.

To begin the lesson, the Common Craft website offers a good introduction to what Twitter is in the video *Twitter in Plain English* (http://commoncraft.com/twitter). Two sites, other than Twitter, that could be used to show example tweets include Historical Tweets (http://historicaltweets.com) and Such Tweet Sorrow (http://www.suchtweetsorrow.com). Historical Tweets is an entertaining site that allows contributors to create tweets from famous people in history. Not all entries are appropriate, so it is best to search the site in advance for good examples and bookmark or copy them to share with students. There are examples of appropriate Historical Tweets on the author's blog. Some examples of people with Historical Tweets include Abraham Lincoln, Neil Armstrong, Harriet Tubman, Anne Frank, and John Hancock. Students would have to understand the famous person's significance in history or know general details about the person to understand the humor of these tweets.

Such Tweet Sorrow is Shakespeare's famous play, *Romeo and Juliet*, performed as tweets from the characters. Students who follow the tweet will be able to read tweets from each character in the story (with each post being 140 characters or fewer, of course) to get the whole story. The Royal Shakespeare Company (RSC) and Mudlark, a mobile entertainment producer, have teamed up to create the site. Of course, students will not be able to read the tweets and avoid Shakespeare's writing all together, but students will be able to engage in active discussions comparing the tweets to the texts for a fuller learning experience.

The teacher and librarian will need to practice reading text as a whole class and summarizing that passage in a succinct way that adheres to the 150-character maximum. Students will need to develop the skills necessary to pick out important points from text and summarize those important points in order to complete this assignment. Students will need to understand the following specifics: writing must be precise and clear; long words should be avoided; information should be implied rather than stated; and declarative sentences and questions are effective ways to communicate. Students will first type all summaries in a document using word processing software to utilize the word count feature and spell-check. Students can then cut and paste their post onto the class wiki.

Since the students will be posting their summaries on a wiki, this lesson requires the librarian or teacher to explain what a wiki is. The Common Craft website offers a good introduction to what a wiki is in the video *Wikis in Plain English* (http://commoncraft.com/video-wikis-plain-english), and the video can also be found on YouTube. This would also be an appropriate time to explain to students the difference between wikis and blogs, so the Common Craft video *Blogs in Plain English* (http://commoncraft.com/blogs) could also be shown to compare and contrast the differences.

The teacher and librarian will show several examples of appropriate grade level book review wikis and blogs and then brainstorm with the students the elements that make a quality book review—plot introduced but not completely revealed, interesting, possibly includes images related to the book (picture of the author, book jacket, or central element from the book), makes you want to read the book, and so on. One example of a book review blog is Guys Lit Wire (http://guyslitwire.blogspot.com). This blog features books that are of interest to teenage boys and is written by a large group of contributors from various demographics and backgrounds including a teacher, a librarian, a book seller, a journalist, and a student. Another example of a blog that focuses on book reviews is Book Nut (http://www.thebooknut.com). The blogger reviews some adult fiction, but the bulk of her posts are for children and young adults. She includes age ranges on each book review she writes. An example of a wiki that focuses on books is Wiki Summaries (http://www.wikisummaries.org). Wiki Summaries is a wiki similar to Wikipedia that allows contributors to submit book summaries. Anyone can contribute by adding summaries, editing summaries, adding additional information to summaries, or commenting on summaries.

The librarian should show some example entries from one of the blogs and from the wiki and a discussion should follow about the differences between a book review and a book summary. The main point that should come out of the discussion is that a book summary reveals the entire plot and conclusion of the book while reviews should provoke the reader to read the book. This lesson could also work as an alternative to a book report by having the students complete the lesson as a summary instead of a book review. After viewing both a blog and a wiki, a discussion should also follow about the major differences between the two different networking mediums. The main point that should come out of the discussion is that blogs may allow users to make comments but have designated writers for the main blog entries while wikis allow users to write and edit entries themselves.

In addition to posting the chapter/section summaries, each student must read at least one other student's posts and make at least two replies to that student. Students should follow these basic guidelines for the appropriate way to reply to a classmate's posts:

1. Compliment the writer, ask a question, or add additional information. Encourage dialogue with your post rather than just a simple statement like "I agree" or "Good job."

2. Only write what you would say in person to your classmates. Never use inappropriate language or state anything that would be insulting or embarrassing to your classmates. Remember, tone and humor can often be misinterpreted, so be sure that posts clearly convey your message.

3. Always use your name so everyone knows who is posting and you get credit for completing the number of required replies.

4. Read over your comment before submitting it. Make sure you are proud of what you wrote before you post. Remember, you are leaving digital footprints every time you post anything. Spelling and grammar are important, so do a quick spell-check before you post.

A rubric given before the project is started will keep students on track and allow students to understand how they will be graded (see the rubric at the end of this lesson plan).

Chapter Summary Example

Your Name: A. Student

Book Title: *The Old Man and the Sea*

Book Author: Ernest Hemingway

Chapter or Page Numbers: Day One

Character Name: Manolin

Manolin	writes
I know Santiago is a good fisherman but my parents don't understand going 84 days without fish so I have no choice but to take a job on another boat.	
	SHARE

Note: Punctuation and spaces between words count as characters.

TABLE 4.2 Book Summary on a Secure Wiki Rubric

Elements	Exemplary 3	Satisfactory but lacking in some areas 2	Needs improvement 1	Score
Summary content	Clear, accurate summary of the book is presented. All summaries are first person from the perspective of the character.	Some information is partially inaccurate or not directly related to the summary of events of the story. Most summaries are first person from the perspective of the character.	Information is incomplete, off topic, or inaccurate. Summaries are not first person from the perspective of the character.	
Creativity	Summaries are original and creative.	Summaries are original but lack some creativity.	Summaries are not original (direct quotes from the book) or lacks creativity.	
Discussion contribution	Posts to classmates add value to the topic discussion. Posts to classmates are written in a way to encourage dialogue and commentary.	Posts to classmates are superficial and do not add direct value to the topic discussion. Most posts to classmates are written in a way to encourage dialogue and commentary.	Posts to classmates are superficial and do not add any value to the topic discussion. Posts to classmates are statements that other users can agree or disagree with but do not encourage dialogue.	
Mechanics	No errors in spelling, grammar, capitalization, or punctuation. Summaries are all less than 150 characters.	Two or fewer errors in spelling, grammar, capitalization, or punctuation. Summaries are all less than 150 characters.	Three or more errors in spelling, grammar, capitalization, or punctuation. Most summaries are over 150 characters.	
Frequency	Exceeds the number of original posts (more than one per chapter or section) and comments to other classmates (more than two).	Meets the minimum number of original posts (one per chapter or section) and comments to other classmates (two).	Does not meet the minimum number of original posts (less than one per chapter or section) and/or comments to other classmates (less than two).	

Total score (out of 15)

Stage Three: Book Summary on Twitter Lesson Plan

Overview

After reading a chapter or section in a book, students will summarize what happened on Twitter in 140 characters or less. Students will write these summaries from the perspective of one of the characters in the book. At the end of the book, the summaries will be read together and should tell the basic story of the whole book. A stage three lesson would require students to use the Twitter website to type their tweets and respond to other members of the class' tweets. All tweets are available on the Internet for everyone to view.

Information and Technology Literacy Standards

NETS5.a Students advocate and practice safe, legal, and responsible use of information and technology.

NETS5.b Students exhibit a positive attitude toward using technology that supports collaboration, learning, and productivity.

NETS5.c Students demonstrate personal responsibility for lifelong learning.

NETS5.d Students exhibit leadership for digital citizenship.

Common Core State Standards

CC.5–8.L.3 Students use knowledge of language and its conventions when writing, speaking, reading, or listening.

CC.7.L.3.a Students choose language that expresses ideas precisely and concisely, recognizing and eliminating wordiness and redundancy.

CC.9–12.L.3 Students apply knowledge of language to understand how language functions in different contexts, to make effective choices for meaning or style, and to comprehend more fully when reading or listening.

CC.5.R.L.2 Students determine a theme of a story, drama, or poem from details in the text, including how characters in a story or drama respond to challenges or how the speaker in a poem reflects upon a topic; summarize the text.

CC.6.R.L.2 Students determine a theme or central idea of a text and how it is conveyed through particular details; provide a summary of the text distinct from personal opinions or judgments.

CC.7.R.L.2 Students determine a theme or central idea of a text and analyze its development over the course of the text; provide an objective summary of the text.

CC.8.R.L.2 Students determine a theme or central idea of a text and analyze its development over the course of the text, including its relationship to the characters, setting, and plot; provide an objective summary of the text.

CC.9–10.R.L.2 Students determine a theme or central idea of a text and analyze in detail its development over the course of the text, including how it

emerges and is shaped and refined by specific details; provide an objective summary of the text.

CC.11–12.R.L.2 Determine two or more themes or central ideas of a text and analyze their development over the course of the text, including how they interact and build on one another to produce a complex account; provide an objective summary of the text.

Resources Needed

Library or classroom book

Computers with Internet access

Networking Media Used

Twitter (http://twitter.com)

Wordle (http://www.wordle.net) or Tagxedo (http://www.tagxedo.com) to create a word cloud of all their tweets

Videos on YouTube (http://www.youtube.com) or Common Craft (http://www.commoncraft.com) to view an introduction to the lesson

Procedures

Students will chose a library book to read on their reading level (or this lesson can be used for a required classroom reading assignment). This lesson requires the teacher and librarian to introduce the Twitter website to the students and work with the students to practice summarizing text in a very concise way. The teacher and librarian will need to practice reading text as a whole class and summarizing the passage in a succinct way that adheres to the 140-character maximum. Students will need to develop the skills necessary to pick out important points from text and summarize those important points in order to complete this assignment. Students will need to understand the following specifics: writing must be precise and clear; long words should be avoided; information should be implied rather than stated; and declarative sentences and questions are some of the most effective ways to tweet.

A discussion should take place to see how familiar students are with Twitter. The librarian should explain that Twitter is a microblogging service and show appropriate examples from the Twitter site to serve as an accurate example for them to model their tweets on. Students will need to learn some of the jargon that is associated with Twitter in order to complete the assignment. Students will need to understand the following terms: Twitter handle and hashtag. Usernames should communicate which character they are representing, and the teacher will assign a unique hashtag to allow easy searching. To begin the lesson, the Common Craft website offers a good introduction to what Twitter is in the video *Twitter in Plain English* (http://commoncraft.com/twitter).

Students will need to register for Twitter and follow the other members of the class. See the handout in the appendix for steps for signing up and following others. All students will share their real name and username with the teacher for identification purposes. The teacher and librarian will follow all the students in the class. In addition to posting the chapter/section summaries, each student will make at least three replies to other students. Students should follow these basic guidelines for the appropriate way to reply to a classmate's posts:

1. Compliment the writer, ask a question, or add additional information. Encourage dialogue with your post rather than just a simple statement like "I agree" or "Good job."

2. Only write what you would say in person to your classmates. Never use inappropriate language or state anything that would be insulting or embarrassing to your classmates. Remember, tone and humor can often be misinterpreted, so be sure that posts clearly convey your message.

3. Always use your name so everyone knows who is posting and you get credit for completing the number of required replies.

4. Read over your comment before submitting it. Make sure you are proud of what you wrote before you post. Remember, you are leaving digital footprints every time you post anything. Spelling and grammar are important, so do a quick spell-check before you post.

A rubric given before the project is started will keep students on track and allow students to understand how they will be graded (see the rubric at the end of this lesson plan).

TABLE 4.3   Twitter Book Summary Rubric

Elements	Exemplary 3	Satisfactory but lacking in some areas 2	Needs improvement 1	Score
Content	Clear, accurate summary of events are presented. All tweets are first person from the perspective of the character. All tweets include the assigned hashtag.	Some information is partially inaccurate or not directly related to the summary of events of the story. Most tweets are first person from the perspective of the character. Most tweets include the assigned hashtag.	Information is incomplete, off topic, or inaccurate. Tweets are not first person from the perspective of the character. Tweets do not include the assigned hashtag.	
Creativity	Tweets are original and creative.	Tweets are original but lack some creativity.	Tweets are not original (retweets or direct quotes from book) and lack creativity.	
Discussion contribution	All tweets are written in a way to encourage dialogue, questions, and commentary.	Most tweets are written in a way to encourage dialogue, questions, and commentary but some tweets are statements that other users can only agree or disagree with.	Tweets are statements that other users can agree or disagree with but do not encourage dialogue.	
Mechanics of tweets	No errors in spelling, grammar, capitalization, or punctuation.	Two or fewer errors in spelling, grammar, capitalization, or punctuation.	Three or more errors in spelling, grammar, capitalization, or punctuation.	
Frequency	Exceeds the number of original tweets (more than one per chapter or section) and comments to other tweets (more than three).	Meets the minimum number of original tweets (one per chapter or section) and comments to other tweets (three).	Does not meet the minimum number of original tweets (less than one per chapter or section) and comments to other tweets (less than three).	

Total score (out of 15)

A good extension activity is to have students use Wordle (http://www.wordle. net) or Tagxedo (http://www.tagxedo.com) to create a word cloud of all their tweets. The word cloud is a good way to visually display the key concepts in the summaries.

Lesson Plans Adapted for Other Subjects

Use subject area learning standards to summarize informational textbook readings. The exact same lesson plans can be used except with sections of the textbook as the assigned reading. After reading an assigned chapter or section in the textbook, students will summarize the major concepts in 140 characters or fewer.

Use foreign language learning standards to have students tweet in a different language. This lesson would provide support for students to learn to converse in a foreign language. Students would be required to have a two-way conversation about an assigned topic with each student posting a comment in 140 characters or fewer.

Use subject area learning standards for new vocabulary development and word definition in each subject area. A student describes a word in 140 characters or fewer and other students guess the word. This lesson can be used in every subject area.

Have Student Complete a KWL (What I Know/ What I Want to Know/What I Learned) Chart on Twitter

What I know: Students can tweet any information they already know about a subject so that the teacher can assess prior knowledge. These short, concise posts allow the teacher to quickly see where learning gaps or misconceptions might exist.

What I want to know: Students can communicate their learning desires with their teacher by posting a tweet about what they would like to learn in class next. These short, concise posts allow the teacher to plan lessons that will engage students through their desire to learn the information and empower the students through the knowledge that they have a say in what they learn.

What I learned: Students can summarize what they learned in class by using the following scenario: "Your friend was absent from class today and you want to make sure he/she knows what was missed, so post a tweet to summarize what you learned in class today." These short, concise posts

---

Twitter Hashtags

Following are some hashtags that apply to our profession to make searching Twitter easier:

Collaboration—#TUcollab

Cyber safety—#cybersafety

Education—#edchat, #teach, #teacher, #education

Education Nation (MSNBC series)—#educationnation

Education policy—#edpolicy

Education reform—#edreform

Future of education—#TUfuture

Global education—#flatclassroom

Information literacy—#infolit

Libraries—#library,   #teacher-librarian,   #followalibrarian, #librarians, #tlchat

Literacy—#literacy

Online learning—#onlinelearning

Professional book recommendations—#TUpdbks

Reading—#readers, #reading, #litchat, #titletalk

Social media—#smchat

Software applications in education—#edapp

Technology integration in education—#edtech, #tech, #technology, #TUtin

Web 2.0 use in education—#web20chat

Writing instruction—#TUwrit

Young adult literature—#yalitchat

---

allow the teacher to quickly see where learning gaps or misconceptions might exist so that the information can be retaught, if necessary.

Twitter Resources

With millions of users out there, it is hard to know who to follow on Twitter for the most relevant information. Table 4.4 is a list of compiled Twitter users who tweet about books and specific library information that you may want to consider subscribing to.

Table 4.5 is a list of compiled Twitter users who tweet instructional technology information that you may want to consider subscribing to.

TABLE 4.4

Twitter Handle	Who They Are and What They Do
aasl	American Association of School Librarians: School library views, news, and book reviews
ALALibrary	American Library Association: Library views, news, and book reviews
cybils	Children's and Young Adults' Bloggers' Literary Awards
davidloertscher	David Loertscher: Former school librarian and current professor of library and information science, researcher, writer, and advocate for school libraries
harperteen	Teen division of HarperCollins: Frequent contests, giveaways, and the latest news for young adult readers
joycevalenza	Joyce Valenza: School librarian, writer, and speaker
KirkusReviews	Kirkus Reviews: Reviews of materials from children to adult
librarycongress	Library of Congress: News from one of the largest libraries in the world
LibraryJournal	Library Journal: Library views, news, and book reviews
neilhimself	Neil Gaiman: Newberry Award–winning author
penguinusa	Penguin Group (USA): One of the largest English-language trade book publishers in the world
RossJTodd	Ross J. Todd: Director for the Center for International Scholarship in School Libraries at Rutgers University, researcher, writer, and speaker
SimonTEEN	Simon and Schuster book publisher: Giveaways, contests, and the latest news on young adult books
sljournal	School Library Journal: The latest news in the library field and reviews of books and digital content
yalsa	Young Adult Library Services Association: A world leader in selecting books and media for teens

TABLE 4.5

Twitter Handle	Who They Are and What They Do
AuntyTech	Donna Baumbach: Educator and technology specialist
BlueSkunkBlog	Doug Johnson: Writer, speaker, technology expert, and director of media and technology of Makato Public Schools
coolcatteacher	Vicki Davis: Teacher, instructional technology director, and presenter
dwarlick	David Warlick: Educator, author, speaker, and technology specialist
ericschmidt	Eric Schmidt: CEO of Google with the latest information from the Internet giant
ewanmcintosh	Ewan McIntosh: Education technology consultant
futureofed	Steve Hargadon: Expert in Web 2.0 technology in the classroom
HallDavidson	Hall Davidson: Writer, speaker, and educator with Discovery Education
hdiblasi	Howie DiBlasi: Technology consultant and speaker
Instructify	Free, useful technology for teachers
kanter	Beth Kanter: Blogger and consultant specializing in social media and networks
kathyschrock	Kathy Schrock: District technology education director, speaker, and technology in education expert
mashable	Pete Cashmore: Mashable staff provides news, updates, guides, and resources for web technologies
mcleod	Scott McLeod: Associate professor, writer, and technology expert
suewaters	Sue Waters: Expert in Web 2.0 technology and blogs in education
TEDChris	Chris Anderson: Works for TED (TED = Technology, Entertainment, Design)
tonyvincent	Tony Vincent: Educator, speaker, and expert in technology in education
web20classroom	Steven W. Anderson: Educator, technology expert, speaker, and writer
willrich45	Will Richardson: Writer, speaker, and technology specialist
wiredinstructor	Dennis O'Connor: Educator, consultant, writer, speaker, and technology expert

Stage One: Wiki-Style Book Review Poster Lesson Plan

Overview

After reading a library book, students will create a book review poster on their book. The poster should have space for classmates to comment on the book review similar to the conversation that would be created on a wiki. Stage one users have limited access to technology or the Internet, so technology is usually utilized by the teacher for demonstration and display purposes. To overcome these technology obstacles, this particular lesson requires the teacher or librarian to use the technology for production and the students to only view the technology through a teacher presentation.

Common Core State Standards

CC.5–8.L.3 Students use knowledge of language and its conventions when writing, speaking, reading, or listening.

CC.7.L.3.a Students choose language that expresses ideas precisely and concisely, recognizing and eliminating wordiness and redundancy.

CC.9–12.L.3 Students apply knowledge of language to understand how language functions in different contexts, to make effective choices for meaning or style, and to comprehend more fully when reading or listening.

CC.5.R.L.2 Students determine a theme of a story, drama, or poem from details in the text, including how characters in a story or drama respond to challenges or how the speaker in a poem reflects upon a topic; summarize the text.

CC.6.R.L.2 Students determine a theme or central idea of a text and how it is conveyed through particular details; provide a summary of the text distinct from personal opinions or judgments.

CC.7.R.L.2 Students determine a theme or central idea of a text and analyze its development over the course of the text; provide an objective summary of the text.

CC.8.R.L.2 Students determine a theme or central idea of a text and analyze its development over the course of the text, including its relationship to the characters, setting, and plot; provide an objective summary of the text.

CC.9–10.R.L.2 Students determine a theme or central idea of a text and analyze in detail its development over the course of the text, including how it emerges and is shaped and refined by specific details; provide an objective summary of the text.

CC.11–12.R.L.2 Determine two or more themes or central ideas of a text and analyze their development over the course of the text, including how they interact and build on one another to produce a complex account; provide an objective summary of the text.

Resources Needed

Library or classroom book

Poster board, paper, glue, markers/crayons, pens/pencils, scissors, and magazines to cut pictures from

Networking Media Used

Children's Books Wiki (http://childrensbooks.wikia.com/wiki/Children%27s_Books_Wiki) and Wiki Summaries (http://www.wikisummaries.org) to show examples of wiki book reviews and summaries

Wikipedia (http://wikipedia.org) or another site to show as an example of a popular, successful wiki

Videos on YouTube (http://www.youtube.com) or Common Craft (http://www.commoncraft.com) to view an introduction to the lesson

Flickr (http://www.flickr.com) to share pictures of the students' finished products

Procedures

Students will chose a library book to read on their reading level (or this lesson can be used for a required classroom reading assignment). This lesson requires the librarian or teacher to explain what a wiki is. To begin the lesson, the Common Craft website offers a good introduction to what a wiki is in the video *Wikis in Plain English* (http://commoncraft.com/video-wikis-plain-english), and their video can also be found on YouTube. The librarian should also show a few examples of some popular wikis that the students might already be familiar with, such as Wikipedia (http://wikipedia.org). The teacher and/or librarian will show several examples of appropriate grade level wiki book reviews and then brainstorm with the students the elements that make a quality book review—plot introduced but not completely revealed, interesting, possibly contains images related to the book (picture of the author, book jacket, or central element from the book), makes you want to read the book, and so on. One example of a wiki with book reviews is Children's Books Wiki (http://childrensbooks.wikia.com/wiki/Children%27s_Books_Wiki). Children's Books Wiki is a wiki that allows anyone to contribute to the site by adding reviews, editing reviews, adding additional information to reviews, or commenting on reviews. Each book has a description, readers' reviews, guidance on content, recommended reading age, and links to other similar books. Books reviewed on the site include children's through young adult books. Another example of a wiki that focuses on books is Wiki Summaries (http://www.wikisummaries.org). Wiki Summaries is a wiki similar to Wikipedia that allows contributors to submit book summaries. Anyone can contribute by adding summaries, editing summaries, adding additional information to summaries, or commenting on summaries. The librarian should show some example entries from both sites and discussion should follow about the differences between a book review and a book summary. The main point that should come out of the discussion is that a book summary reveals the entire plot and conclusion of the book while reviews leave the reader wanting to read the book. This lesson could also work as an alternative to a book report by having the students complete a summary instead of a review.

While viewing examples of wikis, the teacher and librarian should make a point to discuss how conversations are carried out on a wiki. People will post information on a wiki and then other contributors will edit, add to, or comment on that original post. Part of this lesson is preparing students to participate in an online community, so students will need to follow simple guidelines for responding to a classmate's book review.

How to Post a Quality Comment on Someone's Book Review Poster

1. Compliment the writer, ask a question, or add additional information. Encourage dialogue with your post rather than just a simple statement like "I agree" or "Good job."

2. Only write what you would say in person to your classmates. Never use inappropriate language or state anything that would be insulting or

embarrassing to your classmates. Remember, tone and humor can often be misinterpreted, so be sure that posts clearly convey your message.

3. Always use your name so everyone knows who is writing the response and you get credit for completing the number of required replies.

4. Make sure you are proud of what you wrote. Remember, others will see your post. Spelling and grammar are important.

After reading their chosen library books, students will organize their ideas by summarizing the book by writing four brief statements that include these elements:

1. Identification of the main character(s)

2. Outline of the major story plot

3. Identification of the setting and time period of the story

4. Identification of the major themes of the story

Students will then write a short book review that is similar in style to the wikis shown in class. The book review should provide text that hooks readers to want to read the book themselves. The poster must also state that the book is available in the library (for example "Check out this gripping novel now available at your library").

The students will write these book reviews in the center of a poster board with space around the review for classmates to comment on the review—similar to how many people contribute to a wiki. See the template and example at the end of the lesson plan. Each student will be required to respond to at least two other classmates' book reviews. Part of this lesson is preparing students to participate in an online community, so students will need to follow simple guidelines for responding to a classmate's book review.

TABLE 4.6 Wiki-Style Book Review Poster Template

TABLE 4.7 Wiki-Style Book Review Poster Example

| I loved *The Hunger Games* and I have been looking for something similar to it. Thanks for the recommendation.
Ella | This sounds like the dystopian societies that we learned about in class. Is that what you thought when you read it?
Jake | This book sounds awesome.
Carson | I don't like really graphic horror stories so I am not sure if I want to read this book. Can you compare the scare level of this book to a popular movie or other book?
Lyla |

(continued)

TABLE 4.7 Wiki-Style Book Review Poster Example *(continued)*

I am glad I read the review so that I won't waste my time checking it out. I don't like science fiction stuff. Amanda	*The Maze Runner* by James Dashner Review by A. Student If you liked *The Hunger Games* by Suzanne Collins you will love *The Maze Runner* by James Dashner. This book is guaranteed to keep you reading from the very first sentence. Thomas wakes up in "the Glade" not knowing who he is, where he is, or anything else. Thomas has no memories except what his first name is. The Glade is a society of about a hundred teenage boys who live in a gigantic, ever-changing, deadly maze. Every 30 days a new boy arrives in the Glades, but the night after Thomas arrives everything changes when a girl is found who has a mysterious message for the boys. Creatures called "Grievers" stalk the boys and are sure to scare any reader during the many graphic, action-packed scenes in the book. Grab this intense science fiction novel at your library to find out: Will Thomas remember who he is? Will the boys figure out what the message means? Will the boys ever make it out of the maze alive?	I can't wait to read this book to see if Thomas makes it out of the maze. Alyssa
Great review. I was thinking about checking it out and now I know I will for sure. Jesse		Is this book part of a series or is it a single book? Jason

This book sounds like it would make a great movie because of all the action! Mimi	Do you know anything about the author? Have you read any of his other books? Margaret	This book sounds similar to *Lord of the Flies* in some ways. Bill	Your questions really have me wanting to check out this book to find the answers. Jamie

TABLE 4.8 Wiki-Style Book Review Poster Rubric

Elements	Exemplary 3	Satisfactory but lacking in some areas 2	Needs improvement 1	Score
Book hook	Text on the poster clearly and accurately represents the book with sufficient detail to hook a reader. All details of the book are provided without giving away the climax or ending.	Text on the poster is not a completely accurate representation of the book, not clearly presented, or presented in a way that spoils part of the story for a reader by giving away too many details.	Text on the poster is incomplete, off topic, inaccurate, or presented in a way that spoils part of the story for a reader by giving away too many details.	
Organization	The poster is attractive to look at. The poster is neat and organized in design and layout.	The poster is acceptably attractive though it may be a bit unorganized in places or look a little messy.	The organization of the poster and/or its design makes it distracting to look at or unattractive.	
Mechanics	All text is legible and easy to read. There are no grammatical or spelling mistakes on the poster.	Most of the text is legible and easy to read. There are one or two grammatical and/or spelling mistakes on the poster.	The text is illegible or otherwise hard to read. There are three or more grammatical and/or spelling mistakes on the poster.	

TABLE 4.8 Wiki-Style Book Review Poster Rubric *(continued)*

Elements	Exemplary 3	Satisfactory but lacking in some areas 2	Needs improvement 1	Score
Overall construction	Book title and author are clearly identified. All the space on the poster board is used efficiently. Poster shows creativity and originality. Poster entices people to check out the book. Poster clearly states that the book can be checked out from the library.	Book title is clearly identified but author is not. Most of the space on the poster board is used efficiently. Poster shows some creativity and originality but needs improvement. Poster encourages the reader to get the book but does not state that it is available in the library.	Book title and author are not clearly identified. The space on the poster board is either very cluttered or there is too much empty space. Poster lacks creativity and originality. The poster does not encourage other people to want to the read the book. Poster does not state that the book can be checked out from the library.	
Discussion participation	Reads and comments on at least three book reviews. Comments are appropriate and show respect for the work of others.	Reads and comments on two book review. Comments are appropriate and show respect for the work of others.	Did not post comments to other's book reviews or comments are not high quality.	

Total score (out of 15)

Stage Two: Book Review on a Secure Wiki Lesson Plan

Overview

After reading a library book, students will create a book review on their book on a private educational wiki. The students will also be required to comment on their classmates' book reviews on the wiki. A stage two lesson would require students to use the computer to create their book review on the wiki. This is a stage two lesson because the wiki is a private area that is only viewable by the teacher and the students in the class.

Information and Technology Literacy Standards

NETS5.a Students advocate and practice safe, legal, and responsible use of information and technology.

NETS5.b Students exhibit a positive attitude toward using technology that supports collaboration, learning, and productivity.

NETS5.c Students demonstrate personal responsibility for lifelong learning.

NETS5.d Students exhibit leadership for digital citizenship.

Common Core State Standards

CC.5–8.L.3 Students use knowledge of language and its conventions when writing, speaking, reading, or listening.

CC.7.L.3.a Students choose language that expresses ideas precisely and concisely, recognizing and eliminating wordiness and redundancy.

CC.9–12.L.3 Students apply knowledge of language to understand how language functions in different contexts, to make effective choices for meaning or style, and to comprehend more fully when reading or listening.

CC.5.R.L.2 Students determine a theme of a story, drama, or poem from details in the text, including how characters in a story or drama respond to challenges or how the speaker in a poem reflects upon a topic; summarize the text.

CC.6.R.L.2 Students determine a theme or central idea of a text and how it is conveyed through particular details; provide a summary of the text distinct from personal opinions or judgments.

CC.7.R.L.2 Students determine a theme or central idea of a text and analyze its development over the course of the text; provide an objective summary of the text.

CC.8.R.L.2 Students determine a theme or central idea of a text and analyze its development over the course of the text, including its relationship to the characters, setting, and plot; provide an objective summary of the text.

CC.9–10.R.L.2 Students determine a theme or central idea of a text and analyze in detail its development over the course of the text, including how it emerges and is shaped and refined by specific details; provide an objective summary of the text.

CC.11–12.R.L.2 Determine two or more themes or central ideas of a text and analyze their development over the course of the text, including how they interact and build on one another to produce a complex account; provide an objective summary of the text.

Resources Needed

Library or classroom book

Computers with Internet access

Networking Media Used

Children's Books Wiki (http://childrensbooks.wikia.com/wiki/Children%27s_ Books_Wiki) and Wiki Summaries (http://www.wikisummaries.org) to show examples of wiki book reviews and summaries

Wikipedia (http://en.wikipedia.org) or other site to show as an example of a popular, successful wiki

Videos on YouTube (http://www.youtube.com) or Common Craft (http://www.commoncraft.com) to view an introduction to the lesson

PBworks (http://pbworks.com) or Wikispaces for Teachers (http://www.wikispaces.com/content/for/teachers) to post book reviews to a private site that can only be viewed and edited by the teacher and students in the class

Procedures

Students will chose a library book to read on their reading level (or this lesson can be used for a required classroom reading assignment). This lesson requires the librarian or teacher to explain what a wiki is. The Common Craft website offers a good introduction to what a wiki is in the video *Wikis in Plain English* (http://com moncraft.com/video-wikis-plain-english), and their video can also be found on YouTube. The librarian should also show a few examples of some popular wikis that the students might already be familiar with, such as Wikipedia (http://wiki pedia.org). The teacher and/or librarian will show several examples of appropriate grade level wiki book reviews and then brainstorm with the students the elements that make a quality book review—plot introduced but not completely revealed, interesting, possibly contains images related to the book (picture of the author, book jacket, or central element from the book), makes you want to read the book, and so on.

One example of a wiki with book reviews is Children's Books Wiki (http:// childrensbooks.wikia.com/wiki/Children%27s_Books_Wiki). Children's Books Wiki is a wiki that allows anyone to contribute to the site by adding reviews, edit- ing reviews, adding additional information to reviews, or commenting on reviews. Each book has a description, readers' reviews, guidance on content, recommended reading age, and links to other similar books. Books reviewed on the site include children's through young adult books. Another example of a wiki that focuses on books is Wiki Summaries (http://www.wikisummaries.org). Wiki Summaries is a wiki similar to Wikipedia that allows contributors to submit book summa- ries. Anyone can contribute by adding summaries, editing summaries, adding ad- ditional information to summaries, or commenting on summaries. The librarian should show some example entries from both sites and discussion should follow about the differences between a book review and a book summary. The main point that should come out of the discussion is that a book summary reveals the entire plot and conclusion of the book while reviews leave the reader wanting to read the book. This lesson could also work as an alternative to a book report by having the students complete a summary instead of a review.

While viewing examples of wikis, the teacher and librarian should make a point to discuss how conversations are carried out on a wiki. People will post information on a wiki and then other contributors will edit, add to, or comment on that original post. The teacher or librarian will set up a private class wiki and allow all students in the class access to view and edit all the pages. See the appen- dix for handouts with instructions for signing up for PBworks and Wikispaces accounts.

After reading their chosen library books, students will organize their ideas by summarizing the book by writing four brief statements that include these elements:

1. Identification of the main character(s)

2. Outline of the major story plot

3. Identification of the setting and time period of the story

4. Identification of the major themes of the story

Students will then write a short book review that is similar in style to the wikis shown in class. The book review should provide text that hooks readers to want to read the book themselves. The review must also state that the book is available in the library (for example "Check out this riveting read now available at your library").

The students will type their book reviews on the assigned private class wiki page. Students will also be required to read and comment on at least three of their classmates' book reviews. Part of this lesson is preparing students to participate in an online community, so students will need to follow simple guidelines for responding to a classmate's book review.

How to Post a Quality Comment on a Wiki

1. Compliment the writer, ask a question, or add additional information. Encourage dialogue with your post rather than just a simple statement like "I agree" or "Good job."

2. Only write what you would say in person to your classmates. Never use inappropriate language or state anything that would be insulting or embarrassing to your classmates. Remember, tone and humor can often be misinterpreted, so be sure that posts clearly convey your message.

3. Always use your name so everyone knows who is posting and you get credit for completing the number of required replies.

4. Read over your comment before submitting it. Make sure you are proud of what you wrote before you post. Remember, you are leaving digital footprints every time you post anything. Spelling and grammar are important, so do a quick spell-check before you post.

A rubric given before the project is started will keep students on track and allow students to understand how they will be graded (see the rubric at the end of this lesson plan).

TABLE 4.9 Wiki-Style Book Review Rubric

Elements	Exemplary 3	Satisfactory but lacking in some areas 2	Needs improvement 1	Score
Basic information content	Clearly and accurately summarizes the central plot of the book with sufficient detail without giving away the climax or ending. The book summary has a minimum of all four of these elements: identification of the main character(s), outline of the major story plot, identification of the setting and/or time period of the story, and identification of the major themes of the story.	Summary of the central plot is not completely accurate, not clearly presented, or presented in a way that spoils part of the story for a reader by giving away too many details. Information is missing one or two of these elements: identification of the main character(s), outline of the major story plot, identification of the setting and/or time period of the story, or identification of the major themes of the story.	Summary of the central plot is incomplete, off topic, inaccurate, or presented in a way that spoils part of the story for a reader by giving away too many details. Information is missing three or four of these elements: identification of the main character(s), outline of the major story plot, identification of the setting and/or time period of the story, or identification of the major themes of the story.	
Organization	Clear, accurate information is presented. Thoughts are organized and flow smoothly.	Some basic information is not accurate or not clearly presented. Thoughts are organized.	Basic information is incomplete, off topic, or inaccurate. Little organization to writing.	
Overall construction	Page content is original and creative. No errors in spelling, grammar, capitalization, or punctuation.	Page content is original but lacks some creativity. One or two errors in spelling, grammar, capitalization, or punctuation.	Page content is not original or creative. Three or more errors in spelling, grammar, capitalization, or punctuation.	

TABLE 4.9 **Wiki-Style Book Review Rubric** (*continued*)

Elements	Exemplary	Satisfactory but lacking in some areas	Needs improvement	Score
	3	**2**	**1**	
Discussion participation	Read and commented on at least three book reviews. Exhibits appropriate wiki etiquette and shows respect for the work of others.	Read and commented on two book review. Exhibits appropriate wiki etiquette most of the time and generally shows respect for the work of others.	Did not post comments to other's book reviews. Exhibits no knowledge of wiki etiquette and fails to respect the work of others.	
Total score (out of 12)				

Stage Three: Podcast Book Review on a Public Wiki Lesson Plan

Overview

After reading a library book, students will write a book review on their book and then record it as an audio file to be placed on a public wiki. The students will also be required to post comments on their classmates' book reviews on the wiki. This stage three lesson requires students to use technology to create their book review as an audio file and to place that file on a public wiki. This lesson also requires students to listen to other classmates' book reviews in order to comment on them. This is a stage three lesson because unfiltered access to the wiki is required and the wiki is public, thus creating a large authentic audience for the student's products.

Information and Technology Literacy Standards

NETS5.a Students advocate and practice safe, legal, and responsible use of information and technology.

NETS5.b Students exhibit a positive attitude toward using technology that supports collaboration, learning, and productivity.

NETS5.c Students demonstrate personal responsibility for lifelong learning.

NETS5.d Students exhibit leadership for digital citizenship.

Common Core State Standards

CC.5–8.L.3 Students use knowledge of language and its conventions when writing, speaking, reading, or listening.

CC.7.L.3.a Students choose language that expresses ideas precisely and concisely, recognizing and eliminating wordiness and redundancy.

CC.9–12.L.3 Students apply knowledge of language to understand how language functions in different contexts, to make effective choices for meaning or style, and to comprehend more fully when reading or listening.

CC.6.S.L.5 Students include multimedia components (e.g., graphics, image, music, sound) and visual displays in presentations to clarify information.

CC.7.S.L.5 Students include multimedia components and visual displays in presentations to clarify claims and findings and emphasize salient points.

CC.8.S.L.5 Students include multimedia components and visual displays into presentations to clarify information, strengthen claims and evidence, and add interest.

CC.9–12.S.L.5 Students make strategic use of digital media (e.g., textual, graphical, audio, visual, and interactive elements) in presentations to enhance understanding of findings, reasoning, and evidence and to add interest.

CC.5.R.L.2 Students determine a theme of a story, drama, or poem from details in the text, including how characters in a story or drama respond to challenges or how the speaker in a poem reflects upon a topic; summarize the text.

CC.6.R.L.2 Students determine a theme or central idea of a text and how it is conveyed through particular details; provide a summary of the text distinct from personal opinions or judgments.

CC.7.R.L.2 Students determine a theme or central idea of a text and analyze its development over the course of the text; provide an objective summary of the text.

CC.8.R.L.2 Students determine a theme or central idea of a text and analyze its development over the course of the text, including its relationship to the characters, setting, and plot; provide an objective summary of the text.

CC.9–10.R.L.2 Students determine a theme or central idea of a text and analyze in detail its development over the course of the text, including how it emerges and is shaped and refined by specific details; provide an objective summary of the text.

CC.11–12.R.L.2 Determine two or more themes or central ideas of a text and analyze their development over the course of the text, including how they interact and build on one another to produce a complex account; provide an objective summary of the text.

Resources Needed

Library or classroom book

Computers with Internet access

Written script—Paper, pens/pencils

Microphone

Additional Information about Recording Audio

Professional USB microphones like the Blue Snowball Microphone (http://www.bluemic.com/snowball) can provide superior audio recording quality for approximately $100, but much cheaper microphones like those available from Walmart (http://www.walmart.com), Amazon (http://www.amazon.com), or Radio Shack (http://www.radioshack.com) for less than $10 also work well.

Networking Media Used

Children's Books Wiki (http://childrensbooks.wikia.com/wiki/Children%27s_Books_Wiki) and Wiki Summaries (http://www.wikisummaries.org) to show examples of wiki book reviews and summaries

Wikipedia (http://en.wikipedia.org) or another site to show as an example of a popular, successful wiki

Videos on YouTube (http://www.youtube.com) or Common Craft (http://www.commoncraft.com) to view an introduction to the lesson

PBworks (http://pbworks.com/) or Wikispaces for Teachers (http://www.wikispaces.com/content/for/teachers) to post book reviews to a private site that can only be viewed and edited by the teacher and students in the class

Vocaroo (http://vocaroo.com), a free online service that allows users to create audio recordings, or Voki (http://www.voki.com), a service that allows users to create animated audio avatars

Quikqr (http://quikqr.com) is a free website that has both a QR code generator and a QR code reader

Procedures

Students will chose a library book to read on their reading level (or this lesson can be used for a required classroom reading assignment). This lesson requires the librarian or teacher to explain what a wiki is. To begin the lesson, the Common Craft website offers a good introduction to what a wiki is in the video *Wikis in Plain English* (http://commoncraft.com/video-wikis-plain-english), and their video can also be found on YouTube. The librarian should also show a few examples of some popular wikis that the students might already be familiar with, such as Wikipedia (http://en.wikipedia.org). The teacher and/or librarian will show several examples of appropriate grade level wiki book reviews and then brainstorm with the students the elements that make a quality book review—plot introduced but not completely revealed, interesting, possibly contains images related to the book (picture of the author, book jacket, or central element from the book), makes you want to read the book, and so on.

One example of a wiki with book reviews is Children's Books Wiki (http://childrensbooks.wikia.com/wiki/Children%27s_Books_Wiki). Children's Books Wiki is a wiki that allows anyone to contribute to the site by adding reviews, editing reviews, adding additional information to reviews, or commenting on reviews. Each book has a description, readers' reviews, guidance on content, recommended reading age, and links to other similar books. Books reviewed on the site include children's through young adult books. Another example of a wiki that focuses on books is Wiki Summaries (http://www.wikisummaries.org). Wiki Summaries is a wiki similar to Wikipedia that allows contributors to submit book summaries. Anyone can contribute by adding summaries, editing summaries, adding additional information to summaries, or commenting on summaries. The librarian should show some example entries from both sites and discussion should follow about the differences between a book review and a book summary. The main point that should come out of the discussion is that a book summary reveals the entire plot and conclusion of the book while reviews leave the reader wanting to read the book. This lesson could also work as an alternative to a book report by having the students complete a summary instead of a review.

While viewing examples of wikis, the teacher and librarian should make a point to discuss how conversations are carried out on a wiki. People will post information on a wiki and then other contributors will edit, add to, or comment on that original post. Part of this lesson is preparing students to participate in an online community, so students will need to follow simple guidelines for responding to a classmate's book review.

How to Post a Quality Comment on a Wiki

1. Compliment the writer, ask a question, or add additional information. Encourage dialogue with your post rather than just a simple statement like "I agree" or "Good job."

2. Only write what you would say in person to your classmates. Never use inappropriate language or state anything that would be insulting or embarrassing to your classmates. Remember, tone and humor can often be misinterpreted, so be sure that posts clearly convey your message.

3. Always use your name so everyone knows who is posting and you get credit for completing the number of required replies.

4. Read over your comment before submitting it. Make sure you are proud of what you wrote before you post. Remember, you are leaving digital footprints every time you post anything. Spelling and grammar are important, so do a quick spell-check before you post.

After reading their chosen library books, students will organize their ideas by summarizing the book by writing four brief statements that include these elements:

1. Identification of the main character(s)

2. Outline of the major story plot

3. Identification of the setting and time period of the story

4. Identification of the major themes of the story

Students will then write a short book review to record as an audio file. The book review should provide text that hooks readers to want to read the book themselves and should also state that the book is available in the library (for example "Check out this mesmerizing novel now available at your library"). Once the students have written their book reviews, they will record the audio using either Vocaroo or Voki. Vocaroo (http://vocaroo.com) is a free online service that allows users to create audio recordings. Voki (http://www.voki.com) is a service that allows users to create animated audio avatars. Both online services allow users to create audio recordings without the need to install any software. All you need to provide is a microphone. Both sites allow you create a recording (and avatar in Voki's case) that can be embedded into wikis, blogs, and websites. Both sites require very little technical skill and make embedding the audio onto the class wiki very simple. See the handouts in the appendix for using both sites and for embedding the files onto the wiki.

The teacher or librarian will set up a public class wiki that will allow anyone to view and edit the pages. See the handouts in the appendix for signing up for free educational accounts using PBworks or Wikispaces for Teachers. Students will also be required to listen to and comment on at least three of their classmates' book reviews. A rubric given before the project is started will keep students on track and allow students to understand how they will be graded (see rubric at the end of the lesson plan).

Extension: QR Codes

Once the students have created their podcast, a QR code can be generated and glued to the inside cover of the book. By scanning these codes with their smartphone, patrons could listen to the podcast to decide if they want to check out the book. See this example podcast for the book *Ophelia* by Lisa M. Klein (http://flashmedia.glynn.k12.ga.us/files/filesystem/Ophelia.wav):

Free websites can be used to generate a QR code within seconds. This QR code was created by Quikqr (http://quikqr.com), a site that has both a free QR code generator and a free QR code reader. A QR code reader app must be installed on smartphones in order to actually scan the bar code. The short, simple directions for generating a QR code using Quikqr are as follows:

1. Go to Quikqr at http://quikqr.com.

2. Enter a URL or text that you want the QR code to direct users to.

3. Hit the "Generate Code" button.

Once the code is generated, it can be saved by clicking the "Save QR Code as a PNG image" button or by entering your email address to have it sent directly to you. Once the code is saved, it can be printed and displayed anywhere—on books, on bulletin boards, on websites, and so forth.

TABLE 4.10   Podcast Book Review Wiki Rubric

Elements	Exemplary 3	Satisfactory but lacking in some areas 2	Needs improvement 1	Score
Book summary content	Clearly and accurately summarizes the book with sufficient detail without giving the climax or ending away. The podcast book review has a minimum of all four of these elements: identification of the main character(s), outline of the major story plot, identification of the setting and/or time period of the story, and identification of the major themes of the story.	Summary information is not completely accurate, not clearly presented, or presented in a way that spoils part of the story for a reader by giving away too many details. Information is missing one or two of these elements: identification of the main character(s), outline of the major story plot, identification of the setting and/or time period of the story, or identification of the major themes of the story.	Summary information is incomplete, off topic, inaccurate, or presented in a way that spoils part of the story for a reader by giving away too many details. Information is missing three or four of these elements: identification of the main character(s), outline of the major story plot, identification of the setting and/or time period of the story, or identification of the major themes of the story.	
Wiki organization	Book title and author are clearly identified. Thoughts are organized and flow smoothly.	Book title is clearly identified but author is not. Thoughts are organized.	Book title and author are not clearly identified. Lacks organization.	
Information delivery	Smooth delivery shows that the script is well rehearsed. Presenter's speech is clear and easily understandable. Correct grammar and proper enunciation is used throughout the podcast. Podcast clearly states that the book can be checked out from the library.	Appears unrehearsed with presenter appearing to struggle with delivery. Occasionally incorrect grammar and/or enunciation are used during the podcast, making it distracting or hard to understand. Podcast encourages the listener to get the book but does not state that it is available in the library.	Either no script is used or script is unrehearsed, resulting in choppy, unorganized delivery. Poor grammar and enunciation are used throughout the podcast, making it hard to listen to and understand. Podcast does not state that the book can be checked out from the library.	

Technical production	Presentation is recorded in a quiet environment without background noise and distractions. Transitions are smooth. Podcast length keeps the audience interested and engaged. Podcast was uploaded to the assigned wiki.	Presentation is recorded in a semi-quiet environment with some background noise and distractions. Transitions are uneven. Podcast length is too long or too short to keep audience engaged. Podcast was uploaded to the assigned wiki.	Presentation is recorded in a noisy environment with constant background noise and distractions. Transitions are abrupt or too lengthy, making them distracting. Podcast is either too long or too short to keep the audience engaged. Podcast was not uploaded to the assigned wiki.
Overall construction	Creativity and originality enhance the listening experience. Clear, accurate information is presented in an entertaining way. Podcast engages the audience in an entertaining way. Able to hook a reader to check out the book.	Shows some creativity and originality but needs improvement to draw the listener in. Podcast does not engage or entertain the audience as much as it could.	Lacks creativity and originality, which makes the podcast boring or not engaging. Does not encourage other people to want to the read the book.
Discussion participation	Listened to and commented on at least three book reviews. Exhibits appropriate wiki etiquette when posting and shows respect for the work of others.	Listened to and commented on two book review. Exhibits appropriate wiki etiquette most of the time and generally shows respect for the work of others.	Did not post comments to other's book reviews. Exhibits no knowledge of wiki etiquette and fails to respect the work of others.
Total score (out of 18)			

Lesson Plans Adapted for Other Subjects

Foreign language students can create a student wiki in the language that they are studying. Students can interview people in the language that they are studying and embed that interview, as a podcast, on their wiki. They can choose to interview each other, their family members, their friends, or any other community member who proficiently speaks that language.

Students in social studies classes can create a wiki about a significant historical local event. Students can conduct first-person interviews with someone who was present during that event. Students can then embed that interview, as a podcast, on their wiki.

Technology/career prep students can research a career of their choice and then create a wiki to share all the information they discovered about that career including education level required, salary statistics, average workload expected, future job outlook, and so on. Students can conduct first-person interviews with someone who is currently working in their chosen career. Students can then embed that interview, as a podcast, on their wiki.

Students in math classes can create a wiki with podcasts of them as famous mathematicians. The podcasts can be set up in an interview format or a format of the mathematician presenting his or her work at a conference. This lesson can also be adapted to be used with scientists, historical figures, artists, musicians, and more.

Students in music classes can create a wiki to embed recordings of their performances, in the form of podcasts.

5

Social Networking Sites
in the Classroom

Why Use Social Sites?

Some of the most popular networking sites, such as Facebook and Myspace, started as sites used strictly to socialize with others. The basis of a social networking site is to provide an online community with the intent of building relationships among people with similar interests. Because of the social aspect of sites like Facebook and Myspace, most schools consider these sites inappropriate for the school setting and make sure they are blocked by the Internet filter. But these are the sites that students are using every day and get excited about using.

From the growing number of subscribers to social networking sites it seems this trend will continue, so if you want to reach your patrons you will need to use the resources that they use. That is why Facebook is the focus of the lessons in this chapter. There are thousands of social networking sites to choose from, but Facebook has set itself apart from the others and has become a global giant in the field. Facebook recently passed Google statistically as the place where people spend their time on the Internet. Ipsos, a global survey-based market research company, found that three-quarters of teens have a Facebook page. Furthermore, the survey indicated that 65 percent of teens who can access the Internet through their mobile device are continuous Facebook users. Ipsos also found that 56 percent of parents use Facebook and Twitter, while only 27 percent visit their children's school website for information. These statistics show that more patrons could be reached through the use of a social networking site.

Used as a communication tool, Facebook provides the opportunity to increase awareness of your library and thus increase involvement. Facebook increases bonds with the community, builds personal relationships, and offers a sense of belonging for patrons. Engagement, creativity, and innovation are not often equated with Facebook, but they should be. People think of Facebook as a waste of time, but educational Facebook pages represent learning spaces that are both social and student owned. Although Facebook is currently dominating the social networking arena, that may not always be the case. The basis of these lessons can be used on a social networking site that your patrons prefer.

Social Networking Sites Lesson Plans

The following lesson plans incorporate social networking sites, such as Myspace and Facebook, to share information, pictures, and videos. The three stages of lesson plans allow anyone to incorporate the idea of social networking sites into their classroom regardless of technology restrictions.

Stage One: Book Summary Character Profile on Paper Lesson Plan

Overview

Students will check out a library book on their reading level or have a book assigned for classroom reading. Students will create a profile page for one of the characters in the book. As the students are reading

---

Terms to Know

Facebook fans—Facebook users can become fans of your organization by choosing to "like" your organization on your Facebook page. Fans will see notifications you post.

Friends—An option on many social networking sites that allows users who have accepted your invitation or invited you to be connected via the website. When you add someone as a friend, you allow them access to your profile, your wall, and your photos and gain the ability to send them messages.

Like—A Facebook feature that allows people to acknowledge that they like something—a photo, a note, a status post, or an organization.

Profile—The area on a social networking site that allows users to post personal information, such as name, contact information, background information, and pictures.

Status updates—An option on many social networking sites, such as Facebook and Myspace, that allows users to inform their friends of their whereabouts and actions.

Wall—The area on Facebook where people post comments and share photos, videos, and links.

their chapters or sections, they will summarize what happened in a brief statement from the perspective of their chosen character in the book. These summaries will appear as "activity updates" on their profile page. At the end of the book, the activity updates/summaries should tell the basic story of the whole book. Stage one users have limited access to technology or the Internet, so technology is usually utilized by the teacher for demonstration and display purposes. To overcome these technology obstacles, this particular lesson requires the teacher or librarian to use the technology for production and the students to only view the technology through a teacher presentation.

Common Core State Standards

CC.5–8.L.3 Students use knowledge of language and its conventions when writing, speaking, reading, or listening.

CC.7.L.3.a Students choose language that expresses ideas precisely and concisely, recognizing and eliminating wordiness and redundancy.

CC.9–12.L.3 Students apply knowledge of language to understand how language functions in different contexts, to make effective choices for meaning or style, and to comprehend more fully when reading or listening.

CC.5.R.L.2 Students determine a theme of a story, drama, or poem from details in the text, including how characters in a story or drama respond to challenges or how the speaker in a poem reflects upon a topic; summarize the text.

CC.6.R.L.2 Students determine a theme or central idea of a text and how it is conveyed through particular details; provide a summary of the text distinct from personal opinions or judgments.

CC.7.R.L.2 Students determine a theme or central idea of a text and analyze its development over the course of the text; provide an objective summary of the text.

CC.8.R.L.2 Students determine a theme or central idea of a text and analyze its development over the course of the text, including its relationship to the characters, setting, and plot; provide an objective summary of the text.

CC.9–10.R.L.2 Students determine a theme or central idea of a text and analyze in detail its development over the course of the text, including how it

---

Networking Sites to Know

Edmodo (http://www.edmodo.com) is a website that hosts a social learning community that has a similar interface to Facebook or Myspace. Users can create profiles and interact with others through the site. Students can submit assignments for teachers to grade and view grades. Teachers can post grades and assign homework to students.

Facebook (http://www.facebook.com) is one of the most popular social networking sites. Users can create a personal profile, add other users as friends, post status updates to share information with others, comment on friends' status updates, share pictures and videos, and exchange private messages with other users. Registered users must be at least 13 years old.

Myspace (http://www.myspace.com) is a popular social networking site. Users can create a personal profile, add other users as friends, post pictures, and exchange messages. Registered users must be at least 13 years old.

Ning (http://www.ning.com) is an online platform for people to create their own social networks. Ning is no longer a free service, but there is a 30-day free trial and three different levels of paid accounts to choose from. Registered users must be at least 13 years old.

Other Websites Used in the Lessons

Tagxedo (http://www.tagxedo.com) is a free website that generates a visual word cloud, in the shape of a customized image of the user's choice, of text that a user provides. The word cloud image gives greater prominence to words that appear more frequently in the source text to allow a viewer to see the dominant concepts of the text easily.

Wordle (http://www.wordle.net) is a free website that generates a visual word cloud of text that a user provides. The word clouds give greater prominence to words that appear more frequently in the source text to allow a viewer to see the dominant concepts of the text easily. Users can manipulate the fonts, layouts, and color schemes of the word clouds.

emerges and is shaped and refined by specific details; provide an objective summary of the text.

CC.11–12.R.L.2 Determine two or more themes or central ideas of a text and analyze their development over the course of the text, including how they interact and build on one another to produce a complex account; provide an objective summary of the text.

CC.7–8.W.3.a Students engage and orient the reader by establishing a context and introducing a narrator and/or characters; organize an event sequence that unfolds naturally and logically.

CC.7–8.W.3.a Students engage and orient the reader by establishing a context and point of view and introducing a narrator and/or characters; organize an event sequence that unfolds naturally and logically.

CC.9–12.W.3.a Students engage and orient the reader by setting out a problem, situation, or observation, establishing one or multiple points(s) of view, and introducing a narrator and/or characters; create a smooth progression of experiences or events.

Resources Needed

Library or classroom book

Character activity template or poster board, glue, markers/crayons, pens/pencils, scissors, and magazines to cut pictures from

Networking Media Used

Facebook (http://www.facebook.com) or Myspace (http://www.myspace.com) to show students examples of profile pages and status updates so they know what they are expected to do

Videos on YouTube (http://www.youtube.com) or Common Craft (http://www.commoncraft.com) to view an introduction to the lesson

Flickr (http://www.flickr.com) to share pictures of the students' finished products

Procedures

Students will chose a library book to read on their reading level (or this lesson can be used for a required classroom reading assignment). This lesson requires the teacher and/or librarian to introduce social networking websites, such as Facebook and Myspace, to the students. A discussion should take place to see how familiar students are with social networking sites. To begin the lesson, the Common Craft website offers a good introduction to what social networking is in the video *Social Networking in Plain English* (http://commoncraft.com/video-social-networking).

The librarian should show appropriate examples from Facebook, Myspace, or another site that could serve as a model for their profile page. Note: the examples provided in this chapter can be used if these sites are blocked for teacher access. This lesson requires the teacher and librarian to work with the students to practice

MyFace Profile   Home   Personal Info   Photos   Mail (1)   Settings   Log-out

Username:
Page Created by:

| Home | Info | Photos | Mail |

Current Activity:

SHARE

Previous Activity:

Additional Photos (34)

| Personal Information |
| Family: |
| Location: |
| Contacts |

summarizing text in a very concise way. All chapter/section summaries will be just two or three sentences long, so the teacher and librarian will need to practice reading text as a whole class and summarizing that passage in a succinct way. Students will need to develop the skills necessary to pick out important points from text and summarize those important points in order to complete this assignment. Students will need to understand that writing must be precise and clear, long words should be avoided, and some information should be implied rather than stated. The teacher and librarian should also review first-person narratives to ensure students are prepared for the writing task.

Students will use the provided the Character Activity Summary Template (alternatively, students can reproduce the template on a poster board to have a larger display) to write their summaries from the perspective of their chosen character. Students will also draw or paste appropriate pictures on the template for the profile picture, additional pictures, and pictures of contacts. Students should have one profile picture, at least two additional pictures, names and pictures of six contacts, and at least one activity update for each chapter or assigned section of the book.

The character profile pages can be hung in the library, in the classroom, or in prominent places around the building for everyone to see. The teacher or librarian can also take a digital picture of each page to post on a media sharing site, such as Flickr, or the school website. A rubric given before the project is started will keep students on track and allow students to understand how they will be graded (see rubric at the end of the lesson plan).

TABLE 5.1 Character Activity Summary on Paper Rubric

Elements	Exemplary 3	Satisfactory but lacking in some areas 2	Needs improvement 1	Score
Profile page	All required information is filled in (username, profile picture, at least two additional pictures, at least six contacts' names and pictures, and at least 10 activity updates). Page is organized and appealing to look at.	Two to four pieces of required information are missing (username, profile picture, at least two additional pictures, at least six contacts' names and pictures, and at least 10 activity updates). Page is lacking some organization and could be more appealing to look at.	More than five pieces of required information are missing (username, profile picture, at least two additional pictures, at least six contacts' names and pictures, and at least 10 activity updates). Page lacks organization and is not appealing to look at.	
Summary content	Clear, accurate summary of events are presented. Activity updates are original and creative.	Some information is partially inaccurate or not directly related to the summary of events of the story. Activity updates are original but lack some creativity.	Information is incomplete, off topic, or inaccurate. Activity updates are not original (direct quotes from book) and lack creativity.	
Perspective	All activity updates are first person from the perspective of the character. Perspective is accurate for the chosen character.	Most activity updates are first person from the perspective of the character. Perspective is somewhat accurate for the chosen character.	Activity updates are not first person from the perspective of the character. Perspective is not accurate for the chosen character.	
Mechanics of activity updates	Handwriting is legible. No errors in spelling, grammar, capitalization, or punctuation.	Handwriting may be difficult to read in places. Two or fewer errors in spelling, grammar, capitalization, or punctuation.	Handwriting is illegible. Three or more errors in spelling, grammar, capitalization, or punctuation.	

TABLE 5.1   **Character Activity Summary on Paper Rubric** *(continued)*

Elements	Exemplary 3	Satisfactory but lacking in some areas 2	Needs improvement 1	Score
Frequency	Exceeds the number of activity updates required by having at least one update per chapter or assigned section.	Meets the minimum number of activity updates by having only one update per chapter or assigned section.	Does not meet the minimum number of activity updates by having fewer than one update per chapter or assigned section.	

Total score (out of 15)

Stage Two: Book Summary Character Profile Lesson Plan

Overview

The stage one lesson can easily be carried into a stage two lesson plan by having students complete the stage one lesson on the computer. After reading a chapter or section in a book, students will summarize what happened in two to three sentences. Students will write these summaries from the perspective of one of the characters in the book. At the end of the book, the summaries should tell the basic story of the whole book. A stage two lesson would require students to use the computer to type their summaries as activity updates on a template or alternatively on a secure social networking site. A private networking site could only be accessed by the teacher and other members of the class; thus, students would not have access to any information on other social networking sites.

Information and Technology Literacy Standards

NETS5.a Students advocate and practice safe, legal, and responsible use of information and technology.

NETS5.b Students exhibit a positive attitude toward using technology that supports collaboration, learning, and productivity.

NETS5.c Students demonstrate personal responsibility for lifelong learning.

NETS5.d Students exhibit leadership for digital citizenship.

Common Core State Standards

CC.5–8.L.3 Students use knowledge of language and its conventions when writing, speaking, reading, or listening.

CC.7.L.3.a Students choose language that expresses ideas precisely and concisely, recognizing and eliminating wordiness and redundancy.

CC.9–12.L.3 Students apply knowledge of language to understand how language functions in different contexts, to make effective choices for meaning or style, and to comprehend more fully when reading or listening.

CC.5.R.L.2 Students determine a theme of a story, drama, or poem from details in the text, including how characters in a story or drama respond to challenges or how the speaker in a poem reflects upon a topic; summarize the text.

CC.6.R.L.2 Students determine a theme or central idea of a text and how it is conveyed through particular details; provide a summary of the text distinct from personal opinions or judgments.

CC.7.R.L.2 Students determine a theme or central idea of a text and analyze its development over the course of the text; provide an objective summary of the text.

CC.8.R.L.2 Students determine a theme or central idea of a text and analyze its development over the course of the text, including its relationship to the characters, setting, and plot; provide an objective summary of the text.

CC.9–10.R.L.2 Students determine a theme or central idea of a text and analyze in detail its development over the course of the text, including how it emerges and is shaped and refined by specific details; provide an objective summary of the text.

CC.11–12.R.L.2 Determine two or more themes or central ideas of a text and analyze their development over the course of the text, including how they interact and build on one another to produce a complex account; provide an objective summary of the text.

CC.7–8.W.3.a Students engage and orient the reader by establishing a context and introducing a narrator and/or characters; organize an event sequence that unfolds naturally and logically.

CC.7–8.W.3.a Students engage and orient the reader by establishing a context and point of view and introducing a narrator and/or characters; organize an event sequence that unfolds naturally and logically.

CC.9–12.W.3.a Students engage and orient the reader by setting out a problem, situation, or observation, establishing one or multiple points(s) of view, and introducing a narrator and/or characters; create a smooth progression of experiences or events.

CC.6.S.L.5 Students include multimedia components (e.g., graphics, image, music, sound) and visual displays in presentations to clarify information.

CC.7.S.L.5 Students include multimedia components and visual displays in presentations to clarify claims and findings and emphasize salient points.

CC.8.S.L.5 Students include multimedia components and visual displays into presentations to clarify information, strengthen claims and evidence, and add interest.

CC.9–12.S.L.5 Students make strategic use of digital media (e.g., textual, graphical, audio, visual, and interactive elements) in presentations to enhance understanding of findings, reasoning, and evidence and to add interest.

Resources Needed

Library or classroom book

Character Activity Summary Template to edit on the computer

Computers with Internet access

Networking Media Used

Creative Commons (http://search.creativecommons.org) website to find images to use

Edmodo (http://www.edmodo.com), Ning (http://www.ning.com), or class wiki to post book summaries as activity updates that can be viewed by the teacher and students in the class

Videos on YouTube (http://www.youtube.com) or Common Craft (http://www.commoncraft.com) to view an introduction to the lesson

Wordle (http://www.wordle.net) or Tagxedo (http://www.tagxedo.com) to create a word cloud of all their status posts

Procedures

Students will chose a library book to read on their reading level (or this lesson can be used for a required classroom reading assignment). This lesson requires the teacher and librarian to introduce social networking websites, such as Facebook and Myspace, to the students. A discussion should take place to see how familiar students are with social networking sites. To begin the lesson, the Common Craft website offers a good introduction to what social networking is in the video *Social Networking in Plain English* (http://commoncraft.com/video-social-networking).

The librarian should show appropriate examples from Facebook, Myspace, or another site that could serve as a model for their profile page. Note: the examples provided in this chapter can be used if these sites are blocked for teacher access. This lesson requires the teacher and/or librarian to work with the students to practice summarizing text in a very concise way. All chapter/section summaries will be just two or three sentences long, so the teacher and librarian will need to practice reading text as a whole class and summarizing that passage in a succinct way. Students will need to develop the skills necessary to pick out important points from text and to summarize those important points in order to complete this assignment. Students will need to understand that writing must be precise and clear, long words should be avoided, and some information should be implied rather than stated if possible. The teacher and librarian should review first-person narratives to ensure students are prepared for the writing task.

Students will use the provided digital copy of the Character Activity Summary Template to type their summaries from the perspective of their chosen character. Students will search the Creative Commons (http://search.creativecommons.org) website to find images to use on the template for the profile picture, additional pictures, and pictures of contacts. Students should have one profile picture, at least two additional pictures, names and pictures of six contacts, and at least one activity update for each chapter or assigned section of the book.

The profile pages can then be uploaded to a classroom wiki or alternatively the profiles can be completed on a private social networking site, such as Edmodo or Ning (note Ning is now only free for the first 30 days). A rubric given before the project is started will keep students on track and allow students to understand how they will be graded (see rubric at the end of the lesson plan).

Extension: Activity Updates Word Cloud

A good extension activity is to have students use Wordle (http://www.wordle.net) or Tagxedo (http://www.tagxedo.com) to create a word cloud of all their activity posts. The word cloud is a good way to visually display the key concepts in the summaries. See the example word cloud at the end of this lesson plan.

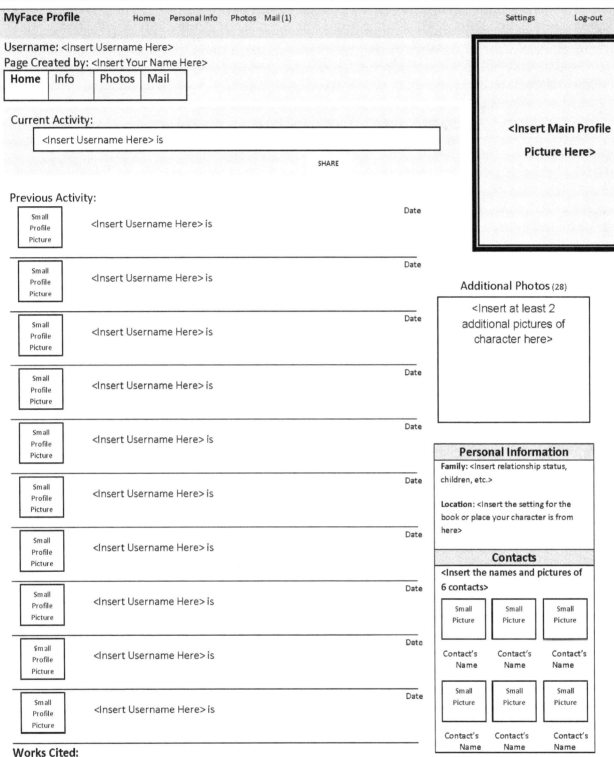

MyFace Profile   Home   Personal Info   Photos   Mail (1)   Settings   Log-out

Username: <Insert Username Here>
Page Created by: <Insert Your Name Here>

| Home | Info | Photos | Mail |

Current Activity:

<Insert Username Here> is

SHARE

Previous Activity:

Small Profile Picture	<Insert Username Here> is	Date
Small Profile Picture	<Insert Username Here> is	Date
Small Profile Picture	<Insert Username Here> is	Date
Small Profile Picture	<Insert Username Here> is	Date
Small Profile Picture	<Insert Username Here> is	Date
Small Profile Picture	<Insert Username Here> is	Date
Small Profile Picture	<Insert Username Here> is	Date
Small Profile Picture	<Insert Username Here> is	Date
Small Profile Picture	<Insert Username Here> is	Date
Small Profile Picture	<Insert Username Here> is	Date

Works Cited:
<Cite all pictures in the proper MLA format here>

<Insert Main Profile Picture Here>

Additional Photos (28)

<Insert at least 2 additional pictures of character here>

Personal Information

Family: <Insert relationship status, children, etc.>

Location: <Insert the setting for the book or place your character is from here>

Contacts

<Insert the names and pictures of 6 contacts>

Small Picture	Small Picture	Small Picture
Contact's Name	Contact's Name	Contact's Name
Small Picture	Small Picture	Small Picture
Contact's Name	Contact's Name	Contact's Name

MyFace Profile Home Personal Info Photos Mail (1)   Settings   Log-out

Username: Daisy Buchanan (From The Great Gatsby by F. Scott Fitzgerald)
Page Created by: A. Student

| **Home** | Info | Photos | Mail |

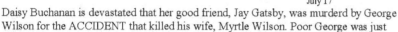

Current Activity:

Daisy Buchanan is packing to move.

SHARE

Previous Activity:

July 17
Daisy Buchanan is devastated that her good friend, Jay Gatsby, was murderd by George Wilson for the ACCIDENT that killed his wife, Myrtle Wilson. Poor George was just insane over the death of his wife and now he murdered Jay and killed himself. It is truly a sad day.

July 10
Daisy Buchanan is lucky to be alive after the terrible car accident I was just in. Sadly, Myrtle Wilson was hit and killed in the accident but thankfully Jay Gatsby and I made it out of the accident with no injuries. Jay feels just awful about Myrtle but accidents do happen and I don't understand why she jumped in front of the car anyway.

July 9
Daisy Buchanan is determined to keep my family together no matter what has happened in the past.

July 9
Daisy Buchanan is stunned to find out that Jay Gatsby is a bootlegger and criminal. I could not believe it when Tom told me.

June 27
Daisy Buchanan is glad to be spending so much time with my old friend, Jay;)

June 21
Daisy Buchanan is furious with Myrtle Wilson. I guess I am the last to find out about the company my husband is keeping. Myrtle needs to find her own man and stay away from mine! Myrtle Wilson, you are nothing but trash.

June 18
Daisy Buchanan is shocked to have run into Jay Gatsby after so many years. Nick should have told me that he also invited Jay to tea so that I was not so surprised.

June 5
Daisy Buchanan is so glad that Nick and Jordan hit it off and are now seeing each other. I hear Nick and Jordan are attending the legendary and extravagant parties at Gatsby's mansion. But new money like Gatsby always tries to be so showy. He sure did not have two pennies to rub together when I knew him in Louisville, Kentucky in 1917. When people come from money, like I do, they don't have to flash their money all around town.

June 4
Daisy Buchanan is thinking about the wonderful dinner I just had with my cousin Nick Carraway, my good friend Jordan Baker, and my husband Tom. I am so glad Nick could come for a visit and Tom was also excited to catch up with his old classmate from Yale.

Additional photos (39)

Personal Information
Family: Married to Tom Buchanan and have a three year old daughter
Location: Currently living in Long Island, New York but originally from Louisville, Kentucky

Contacts

F. Scott Fitzgerald   Jordan Baker   Myrtle Wilson

Jay Gatsby   Tom Buchanan   Nick Carraway

Activity Summary Word Cloud Example Based on Daisy Buchanan from *The Great Gatsby* by F. Scott Fitzgerald

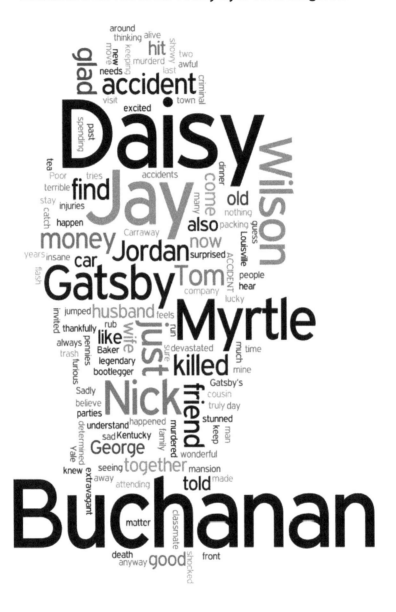

TABLE 5.2   Character Activity Summary Rubric

Elements	Exemplary 3	Satisfactory but lacking in some areas 2	Needs improvement 1	Score
Profile page	All required information is filled in (username, profile picture, at least two additional pictures, at least six contacts' names and pictures, and at least 10 activity updates). Page is organized and appealing to look at.	Two to four pieces of required information are missing (username, profile picture, at least two additional pictures, at least six contacts' names and pictures, and at least 10 activity updates). Page is lacking some organization and could be more appealing to look at.	More than five pieces of required information are missing (username, profile picture, at least two additional pictures, at least six contacts' names and pictures, and at least 10 activity updates). Page lacks organization and is not appealing to look at.	
Summary content	Clear, accurate summary of events are presented. Activity updates are original and creative.	Some information is partially inaccurate or not directly related to the summary of events of the story. Activity updates are original but lack some creativity.	Information is incomplete, off topic, or inaccurate. Activity updates are not original (direct quotes from book) and lack creativity.	
Perspective	All activity updates are first person from the perspective of the character. Perspective is accurate for the chosen character.	Most activity updates are first person from the perspective of the character. Perspective is somewhat accurate for the chosen character.	Activity updates are not first person from the perspective of the character. Perspective is not accurate for the chosen character.	
Mechanics of activity updates	No errors in spelling, grammar, capitalization, or punctuation. All pictures and other text sources are cited properly in MLA format on the page. Profile was uploaded to assigned classroom area.	Two or fewer errors in spelling, grammar, capitalization, or punctuation. All pictures and other text sources are cited, but there are some minor errors in the MLA format. Profile was uploaded to assigned classroom area.	Three or more errors in spelling, grammar, capitalization, or punctuation. No citation provided on the page. Profile was not uploaded to the assigned classroom area.	
Frequency	Exceeds the number of activity updates required by having at least one activity update per chapter or assigned section. Exceeds the number of comments to other classmates' activity updates.	Meets the minimum number of activity updates by having only one activity update per chapter or assigned section. Meets the minimum number the number of comments to other classmates' activity updates.	Does not meet the minimum number of status updates by having fewer than one activity update per chapter or assigned section. Does not meet the minimum number the number of comments to other classmates' activity updates.	

Total score (out of 15)

Stage Three: Book Summary on Facebook Lesson Plan

Overview

The stage two lesson can easily be carried into a stage three lesson plan by having students complete the lesson on a public social networking site. After reading a chapter or section in a book, students will summarize what happened in two to three sentences. Students will write these summaries from the perspective of one of the characters in the book. At the end of the book, the summaries should tell the basic story of the whole book. A stage three lesson would require students to use the Facebook website or a comparable public social networking site. Students will build their chosen character's profile page, friend other classmates, and post all their chapter/section summaries as status posts. All the character profile pages will be available on the Internet for everyone to view.

Information and Technology Literacy Standards

NETS5.a Students advocate and practice safe, legal, and responsible use of information and technology.

NETS5.b Students exhibit a positive attitude toward using technology that supports col-laboration, learning, and productivity.

NETS5.c Students demonstrate personal responsibility for lifelong learning.

NETS5.d Students exhibit leadership for digital citizenship.

Common Core State Standards:

CC.5–8.L.3 Students use knowledge of language and its conventions when writing, speaking, reading, or listening.

CC.7.L.3.a Students choose language that expresses ideas precisely and concisely, recognizing and eliminating wordiness and redundancy.

CC.9–12.L.3 Students apply knowledge of language to understand how language functions in different contexts, to make effective choices for meaning or style, and to comprehend more fully when reading or listening.

CC.5.R.L.2 Students determine a theme of a story, drama, or poem from details in the text, including how characters in a story or drama respond to challenges or how the speaker in a poem reflects upon a topic; summarize the text.

CC.6.R.L.2 Students determine a theme or central idea of a text and how it is conveyed through particular details; provide a summary of the text distinct from personal opinions or judgments.

CC.7.R.L.2 Students determine a theme or central idea of a text and analyze its development over the course of the text; provide an objective summary of the text.

CC.8.R.L.2 Students determine a theme or central idea of a text and analyze its development over the course of the text, including its relationship to the characters, setting, and plot; provide an objective summary of the text.

CC.9–10.R.L.2 Students determine a theme or central idea of a text and analyze in detail its development over the course of the text, including how it emerges and is shaped and refined by specific details; provide an objective summary of the text.

CC.11–12.R.L.2 Determine two or more themes or central ideas of a text and analyze their development over the course of the text, including how they interact and build on one another to produce a complex account; provide an objective summary of the text.

CC.7–8.W.3.a Students engage and orient the reader by establishing a context and introducing a narrator and/or characters; organize an event sequence that unfolds naturally and logically.

CC.7–8.W.3.a Students engage and orient the reader by establishing a context and point of view and introducing a narrator and/or characters; organize an event sequence that unfolds naturally and logically.

CC.9–12.W.3.a Students engage and orient the reader by setting out a problem, situation, or observation, establishing one or multiple points(s) of view, and introducing a narrator and/or characters; create a smooth progression of experiences or events.

CC.6.S.L.5 Students include multimedia components (e.g., graphics, image, music, sound) and visual displays in presentations to clarify information.

CC.7.S.L.5 Students include multimedia components and visual displays in presentations to clarify claims and findings and emphasize salient points.

CC.8.S.L.5 Students include multimedia components and visual displays into presentations to clarify information, strengthen claims and evidence, and add interest.

CC.9–12.S.L.5 Students make strategic use of digital media (e.g., textual, graphical, audio, visual, and interactive elements) in presentations to enhance understanding of findings, reasoning, and evidence and to add interest.

Resources Needed

Library or classroom book

Computers with Internet access

Networking Media Used

Creative Commons (http://search.creativecommons.org) website to find images to use

Facebook (http://www.facebook.com) to post book summaries as status updates

Status Cloud Facebook App (http://statuscloud.icodeforlove.com/?ref=nf) to create a word cloud of all their status posts

Videos on YouTube (http://www.youtube.com) or Common Craft (http://www.commoncraft.com) to view an introduction to the lesson

Procedures

Students will chose a library book to read on their reading level (or this lesson can be used for a required classroom reading assignment). This lesson requires the teacher and/or librarian to introduce social networking websites, such as Facebook and Myspace, to the students. A discussion should take place to see how familiar students are with social networking sites. To begin the lesson, the Common Craft website offers a good introduction to what social networking is in the video *Social Networking in Plain English* (http://commoncraft.com/video-social-networking). The librarian should show appropriate examples from Facebook that could serve as an accurate model for their profile page. Students will need to learn some of the jargon that is associated with social networking sites in order to complete the assignment. Students will need to understand the following terminology: profile, status updates, wall, and friends.

This lesson requires the teacher and librarian to work with the students to practice summarizing text in a very concise way. All chapter/section summaries will be just two or three sentences long, so the teacher and librarian will need to practice reading text as a whole class and summarizing that passage in a succinct way. Students will need to develop the skills necessary to pick out important points from text and to summarize those important points in order to complete this assignment. Students will need to understand that writing must be precise and clear, long words should be avoided, and some information should be implied rather than stated if possible. The teacher and librarian should also review first-person narratives to ensure students are prepared for the writing task.

Students will need to register for Facebook and friend the other members of the class (note: If students already have a Facebook account they will need to sign up for another email account to use for this lesson). Students will need to mark their profile page's privacy settings as accessible by everyone. All students will share their real name and username with the teacher for identification purposes. The teacher and librarian will also friend all the students in the class.

Students will search the Creative Commons (http://search.creativecommons.org/) website to find images to use for the profile picture, additional pictures, and pictures of friends. Students should have one profile picture, at least two additional pictures, names and pictures of six friends, and at least one status update for each chapter or assigned section of the book.

In addition to posting the chapter/section summaries, each student must read at least two other students' status updates and make at least two comments to those student (as their character, of course). A rubric given before the project is started will keep students on track and allow students to understand how they will be graded (see rubric at the end of the lesson plan).

TABLE 5.3   Character Facebook Status Update Rubric

Elements	Exemplary 3	Satisfactory but lacking in some areas 2	Needs improvement 1	Score
Profile page	All required information is filled in (profile picture, at least two additional pictures, at least six friends, and at least 10 status updates).	Two to four pieces of required information are missing (profile picture, at least two additional pictures, at least six friends, and at least 10 status updates).	More than five pieces of required information are missing (profile picture, at least two additional pictures, at least six friends, and at least 10 status updates).	
Summary content	Clear, accurate summary of events is presented. Status updates are original and creative.	Some information is partially inaccurate or not directly related to the summary of events of the story. Status updates are original but lack some creativity.	Information is incomplete, off topic, or inaccurate. Status updates are not original (direct quotes from book) and lack creativity.	
Perspective	All status updates are first person from the perspective of the character. Perspective is accurate for the chosen character.	Most status updates are first person from the perspective of the character. Perspective is somewhat accurate for the chosen character.	Status updates are not first person from the perspective of the character. Perspective is not accurate for the chosen character.	

TABLE 5.3 **Character Facebook Status Update Rubric** *(Continued)*

Elements	Exemplary	Satisfactory but lacking in some areas	Needs improvement	Score
	3	**2**	**1**	
Mechanics of status updates	No errors in spelling, grammar, capitalization, or punctuation. All pictures and other text sources are cited properly in MLA format as a status post on the page. Profile is available for everyone to view on Facebook.	Two or fewer errors in spelling, grammar, capitalization, or punctuation. All pictures and other text sources are cited, but there are some minor errors in the MLA format. Profile is available for viewing on Facebook.	Three or more errors in spelling, grammar, capitalization, or punctuation. No citation provided on the page. Profile was not available for viewing on Facebook.	
Frequency	Exceeds the number of status updates required by having at least one status update per chapter or assigned section. Exceeds the number of required comments (at least two) to other classmates' status updates.	Meets the minimum number of status updates by having only one status update per chapter or assigned section. Meets the minimum number of required comments (exactly two) to other classmates' status updates.	Does not meet the minimum number of status updates by having less than one status update per chapter or assigned section. Does not meet the minimum number of required comments (at least two required) to other classmates' status updates.	
Total score (out of 15)				

Extension: Status Word Cloud

A good extension activity is to have students use the Status Cloud Facebook App (http://statuscloud.icodeforlove.com/?ref=nf) to create a word cloud of all their status posts. The word cloud is a good way to visually display the key concepts in the summaries.

Lesson Plans Adapted for Other Subjects

Use social studies, science, math, art, or mythology learning standards to have students do this exact same lesson except substitute a historian, scientist, mathematician, artist, or god/goddess from mythology for the character. Student can create their activity summaries pages as a historian, scientist, mathematician, artist, or god/goddess from mythology whom they were assigned or chose themselves. The activity posts will consist of major events from that person's life. For example, the famous mathematician Euclid might have the following activity posts: "I spoke with Aristotle today to explain my unique factorization theorem. He was fascinated by my idea that any integer greater than one can be written as a unique product of prime numbers" and "Today I got approval from the great University of Alexandria to open my School of Mathematics. My dream is that one day everyone will study mathematics in school."

Use social studies, science, math, art, or any other subject learning standards to have students summarize textbook readings. Students should pretend to be the textbook author and create summary posts describing why he or she chose to include that information in the textbook. For example, after reading a section on DNA in a science textbook, a student might post "I have just learned that Deoxyribonucleic Acid (DNA) is the basis for the blueprint for all life. This is a must for the textbook because everyone needs to know DNA sequences encode genes. The genes are part of the mechanism that makes a cell function and are responsible for building complex proteins that are used for many purposes such as determining the physical traits of the organism."

Stage One: Profile Page on Paper Lesson Plan

Overview

Students will be assigned or choose a poet, author, or character in a book to create a profile page on that person. Stage one users have limited access to technology or the Internet, so technology is usually utilized by the teacher for demonstration and display purposes. To overcome these technology obstacles, this particular lesson requires the teacher or librarian to use the technology for production and the students to only view the technology through a teacher presentation.

Common Core State Standards

CC.5–8.L.3 Students use knowledge of language and its conventions when writing, speaking, reading, or listening.

CC.7.L.3.a Students choose language that expresses ideas precisely and concisely, recognizing and eliminating wordiness and redundancy.

CC.9–12.L.3 Students apply knowledge of language to understand how language functions in different contexts, to make effective choices for meaning or style, and to comprehend more fully when reading or listening.

CC.7–8.W.3.a Students engage and orient the reader by establishing a context and introducing a narrator and/or characters; organize an event sequence that unfolds naturally and logically.

CC.7–8.W.3.a Students engage and orient the reader by establishing a context and point of view and introducing a narrator and/or characters; organize an event sequence that unfolds naturally and logically.

CC.9–12.W.3.a Students engage and orient the reader by setting out a problem, situation, or observation, establishing one or multiple points(s) of view, and introducing a narrator and/or characters; create a smooth progression of experiences or events.

CC.6–8.W.8 Students gather relevant information from multiple print and digital sources, using search terms effectively; assess the credibility and accuracy of each source; and quote or paraphrase the data and conclusions of others while avoiding plagiarism and following a standard format for citation.

CC.9–10.W.8 Students gather relevant information from multiple authoritative print and digital sources, using advanced searches effectively; assess the usefulness of each source in answering the research question; integrate information into the text selectively to maintain the flow of ideas, avoiding plagiarism and following a standard format for citation.

CC.11–12.W.8 Students gather relevant information from multiple authoritative print and digital sources, using advanced searches effectively; assess the strengths and limitations of each source in terms of the task, purpose, and audience; integrate information into the text selectively to maintain the flow of ideas, avoiding plagiarism and overreliance on any one source and following a standard format for citation.

Resources Needed

Library or classroom book

Template or poster board, glue, markers/crayons, pens/pencils, scissors, and magazines to cut pictures from

Encyclopedias, biographies, and other books to research assigned or chosen person

Networking Media Used

Facebook (http://www.facebook.com) or Myspace (http://www.myspace.com) to show students examples of profile pages and status updates so they know what they are expected to do

Videos on YouTube (http://www.youtube.com) or Common Craft (http://www.commoncraft.com) to view an introduction to the lesson

Flickr (http://www.flickr.com) to share pictures of the students' finished products

Procedures

Students will be assigned or choose a poet, author, or character in a book to create a profile page on that person. This lesson requires the teacher and librarian to introduce social networking websites, such as Facebook and Myspace, to the students. A discussion should take place to see how familiar students are with social networking sites. To begin the lesson, the Common Craft website offers a good introduction to what social networking is in the video *Social Networking in Plain English* (http://commoncraft.com/video-social-networking).

Students will need to learn some of the jargon that is associated with social networking sites in order to complete the assignment. Students will need to understand the following terminology: profile, status updates, wall, and friends. The librarian should show appropriate examples from Facebook that could serve as a model for their profile page. Note: the examples provided in this chapter can be used if these sites are blocked for teacher access.

Students will use encyclopedias, biographies, and other books to research their assigned or chosen person. Students will need to research to find the following information to complete the profile page on their person: name, gender, birthday, hometown, current residence, relationship information, education, occupation, political views, and religious views. Students will also research the person's interest and hobbies in order to draw conclusions about personal information, such as the following: inspirational people; favorite quotations, music, books, movies, television, games, sports, teams, and athletes; activities; and interests. Students will also draw or paste appropriate pictures on the template for the profile picture, additional pictures, and pictures of contacts. Students should have one profile picture, three additional pictures, names and pictures of three contacts, and at least two activity updates.

The profile pages can be hung in the library, in the classroom, or in prominent places around the building for everyone to see. The teacher or librarian can also take a digital picture of each page to post on a media sharing site, such as Flickr, or the school website. A rubric given before the project is started will keep students on track and allow students to understand how they will be graded (see rubric at the end of the lesson plan).

MyFace Profile   Home   Personal Info   Photos   Mail (3)   Settings   Log-out

Username:

Page Created by:

Home	Info	Photos	Mail

Current Activity:

SHARE

Previous Activity:

Basic Information:

Gender:

Birthday:

Hometown:

Current Residence:

Relationship Status:

Education:

Occupation:

Political Views:

Religious Views:

Personal Information:

Activities:

Interests:

Favorite Music:

Favorite TV Shows:

Favorite Movies:

Favorite Books:

Favorite Quotations:

My Favorite Sayings:

Favorite Foods:

How I Spend My Free Time:

About Me:

Additional Photos (27)

Personal Information

Family:

Location:

Contacts

TABLE 5.4   Person Profile Summary Template on Paper Rubric

Elements	Exemplary 3	Satisfactory but lacking in some areas 2	Needs improvement 1	Score
Basic Information Content	Clear, accurate basic information is presented. Information meets the minimum requirement of these ten elements: name, gender, birthday, hometown, current residence, relationship information, education, occupation, political views, and religious views.	Some basic information is not accurate or not clearly presented. Information is missing three to five of the requirement elements. Required elements include name, gender, birthday, hometown, current residence, relationship information, education, occupation, political views, and religious views.	Basic information is incomplete, off topic, or inaccurate. Information is missing six or more of the requirement elements. Required elements include name, gender, birthday, hometown, current residence, relationship information, education, occupation, political views, and religious views.	
Personal Information Content	Clear, accurate information is presented. Information meets the minimum requirement of one of each of these ten elements: activities, interests, type of favorite music, favorite TV show, favorite movie, favorite book, favorite quotation, favorite saying, favorite food, statement about how free time is spent, and an about me statement.	Some basic information is not accurate or not clearly presented. Information is missing three to five of the requirement elements. Required elements include activities, interests, type of favorite music, favorite TV show, favorite movie, favorite book, favorite quotation, favorite saying, favorite food, statement about how free time is spent, and an about me statement.	Basic information is incomplete, off topic, or inaccurate. Information is missing six or more of the requirement elements. Required elements include activities, interests, type of favorite music, favorite TV show, favorite movie, favorite book, favorite quotation, favorite saying, favorite food, statement about how free time is spent, and an about me statement.	
Pictures	Number of pictures meets or exceeds the minimum requirement of seven pictures. Required pictures include one profile picture, three pictures in the photo album with a brief caption, and three contacts' profile pictures with names.	Two or three of the required pictures are missing. Required pictures include: one profile picture, three pictures in the photo album with a brief caption, and three contacts' profile pictures with names.	Four or more of the required pictures are missing. Required pictures include: one profile picture, three pictures in the photo album with a brief caption, and three contacts' profile pictures with names.	
Mechanics	Handwriting is legible. No errors in spelling, grammar, capitalization, or punctuation.	Handwriting may be difficult to read in places. Two or less errors in spelling, grammar, capitalization, or punctuation.	Handwriting is illegible. Three or more errors in spelling, grammar, capitalization, or punctuation.	
Overall construction	Page content is original and creative. All information is filled in, page is organized, and appealing to look at.	Page content is original but lacks some creativity. Some information is missing, page is lacking some organization, and could be more appealing to look at.	Page content is not original or creative. Information is missing, page lacks organization, and is not appealing to look at.	

Total Score (out of 15)

Stage Two: Profile Page Lesson Plan

Overview

Students will be assigned or choose a poet, author, or character in a book to create a profile page on that person. The stage one lesson can easily be carried into a stage two lesson plan by having students complete the stage one lesson on the computer. A stage two lesson would require students to use the computer to type their profile pages on the template or alternatively on a secure social networking site. A private networking site could only be accessed by the teacher and other members of the class; thus, students would not have access to any information on other social networking sites.

Information and Technology Literacy Standards

NETS3.b Students locate, organize, analyze, evaluate, synthesize, and ethically use information from a variety of sources and media.

NETS3.c Students evaluate and select information sources and digital tools based on the appropriateness to specific tasks.

NETS5.a Students advocate and practice safe, legal, and responsible use of information and technology.

NETS5.b Students exhibit a positive attitude toward using technology that supports collaboration, learning, and productivity.

NETS5.c Students demonstrate personal responsibility for lifelong learning.

NETS5.d Students exhibit leadership for digital citizenship.

NETS6.a Students understand and use technology systems.

Common Core State Standards

CC.5–8.L.3 Students use knowledge of language and its conventions when writing, speaking, reading, or listening.

CC.7.L.3.a Students choose language that expresses ideas precisely and concisely, recognizing and eliminating wordiness and redundancy.

CC.9–12.L.3 Students apply knowledge of language to understand how language functions in different contexts, to make effective choices for meaning or style, and to comprehend more fully when reading or listening.

CC.6–8.WH/SS/S/T6 Students use technology, including the Internet, to produce and publish writing and present the relationships between information and ideas clearly and efficiently.

CC.9–10.WH/SS/S/T6 Students use technology, including the Internet, to produce, publish, and update individual or shared writing products, taking advantage of technology's capacity to link to other information and to display information flexibly and dynamically.

CC.11–12.WH/SS/S/T6 Students use technology, including the Internet, to produce, publish, and update individual or shared writing products in response to ongoing feedback, including new arguments of information.

CC.7–8.W.3.a Students engage and orient the reader by establishing a context and introducing a narrator and/or characters; organize an event sequence that unfolds naturally and logically.

CC.7–8.W.3.a Students engage and orient the reader by establishing a context and point of view and introducing a narrator and/or characters; organize an event sequence that unfolds naturally and logically.

CC.9–12.W.3.a Students engage and orient the reader by setting out a problem, situation, or observation, establishing one or multiple points(s) of view, and introducing a narrator and/or characters; create a smooth progression of experiences or events.

CC.6–8.W.8 Students gather relevant information from multiple print and digital sources, using search terms effectively; assess the credibility and accuracy of each source; and quote or paraphrase the data and conclusions of others while avoiding plagiarism and following a standard format for citation.

CC.9–10.W.8 Students gather relevant information from multiple authoritative print and digital sources, using advanced searches effectively; assess the usefulness of each source in answering the research question; integrate information into the text selectively to maintain the flow of ideas, avoiding plagiarism and following a standard format for citation.

CC.11–12.W.8 Students gather relevant information from multiple authoritative print and digital sources, using advanced searches effectively; assess the strengths and limitations of each source in terms of the task, purpose, and audience; integrate information into the text selectively to maintain the flow of ideas, avoiding plagiarism and overreliance on any one source and following a standard format for citation.

CC.6.S.L.5 Students include multimedia components (e.g., graphics, image, music, sound) and visual displays in presentations to clarify information.

CC.7.S.L.5 Students include multimedia components and visual displays in presentations to clarify claims and findings and emphasize salient points.

CC.8.S.L.5 Students include multimedia components and visual displays into presentations to clarify information, strengthen claims and evidence, and add interest.

CC.9–12.S.L.5 Students make strategic use of digital media (e.g., textual, graphical, audio, visual, and interactive elements) in presentations to enhance understanding of findings, reasoning, and evidence and to add interest.

Resources Needed

Library or classroom book

Computers with Internet access

Person Profile Summary Template

Encyclopedias, biographies, and other books to research assigned or chosen person

Facebook (http://www.facebook.com) or Myspace (http://www.myspace.com) to show students examples of profile pages and status updates so they know what they are expected to do

Videos on YouTube (http://www.youtube.com) or Common Craft (http://www.commoncraft.com) to view an introduction to the lesson

Creative Commons (http://search.creativecommons.org) website to find images to use

Edmodo (http://www.edmodo.com), Ning (http://www.ning.com), or class wiki to post book summaries as status updates that can be viewed by the teacher and students in the class

Flickr (http://www.flickr.com)·to share pictures of the students' finished products

Procedures

Students will be assigned or choose a poet, author, or character in a book to create a profile page on that person. This lesson requires the teacher and/or librarian to introduce social networking websites, such as Facebook and Myspace, to the students. A discussion should take place to see how familiar students are with social networking sites. To begin the lesson, the Common Craft website offers a good introduction to what social networking is in the video *Social Networking in Plain English* (http://commoncraft.com/video-social-networking).

Students will need to learn some of the jargon that is associated with social networking sites in order to complete the assignment. Students will need to understand the following terminology: profile, status updates, wall, and friends. The librarian should show appropriate examples from Facebook that could serve as a model for their profile page. Note: the examples provided in this chapter can be used if these sites are blocked for teacher access.

Students will use the Internet and library books to research their assigned or chosen person. Students will need to research to find the following information to complete the profile page on their person: name, gender, birthday, hometown, current residence, relationship information, education, occupation, political views, and religious views. Students will also research the person's interest and hobbies in order to draw conclusions about personal information, such as the following: inspirational people; favorite quotations, music, books, movies, television, games, sports, teams, and athletes; activities; and interests. Students will then use the provided Person Profile Summary Template to record their researched information.

Students will search the Creative Commons (http://search.creativecommons.org) website to find images to use for the profile picture, additional pictures, and pictures of friends. Students should have one profile picture, three additional pictures, names and pictures of three friends, and at least two status updates with smaller profile pictures next to them.

The profile pages can then be uploaded to a classroom wiki or alternatively the profiles can be completed on a private social networking site, such as Edmodo or Ning (note: Ning is now only free for the first 30 days). In addition to their profile page, each student must read at least two other students' profile pages and make

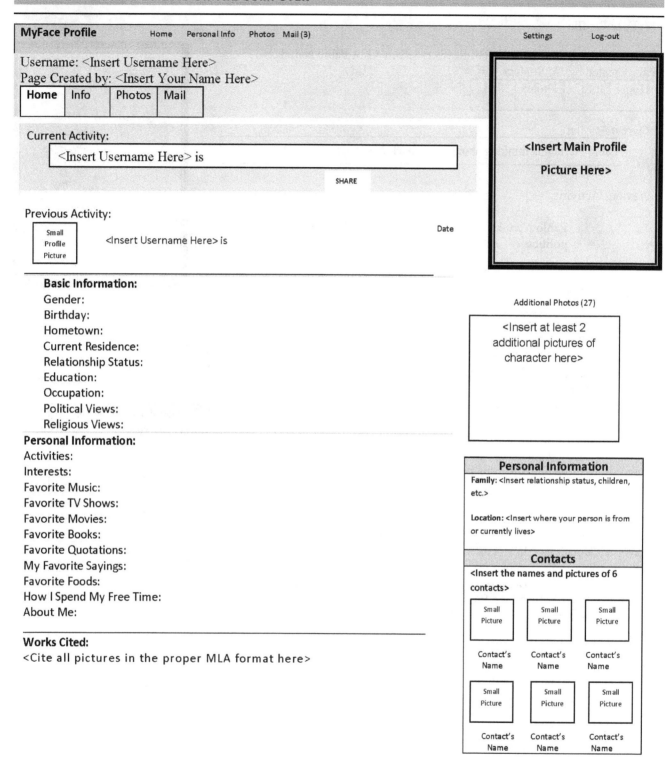

at least two comments to those students (as their assigned person, of course). A rubric given before the project is started will keep students on track and allow students to understand how they will be graded (see rubric at the end of the lesson plan).

MyFace Profile   Home   Personal Info   Photos   Mail (3)   Settings   Log-out

Username: Ricardo Eliecer Neftalí Reyes Basoalto AKA Pablo Neruda
Page Created by: A. Student

Home	Info	Photos	Mail

Current Activity:

> Pablo Neruda is thinking about going back to school.

SHARE

Previous Activity:

February 5

Pablo Neruda is chatting with my friend Gabriela about politics.

Basic Information:
Gender: Male
Birthday: July 12, 1904
Hometown: Parral, Chile
Current Residence: Santiago, Chile
Relationship Status: Married
Education: Dropped out of school at age 12
Occupation: Poet
Political Views: Communist
Religious Views: Catholic

Personal Information:
Activities: Writing poems and serving as a diplomat
Interests: Writing and following politics
Favorite Music: Salsa music and Romantic songs
Favorite TV Shows: *El Humor de Hector Suarez*
Favorite Movies: The great Spanish romance, *Bella*
Favorite Books: My book, *Alturas de Macchu-Picchu*
Favorite Quotations: "In you the wars and the flights accumulated. From you the wings of the song birds rose" (from my poem, *A Song Of Despair*).
My Favorite Sayings: Do what your heart says and do the world a favor.
Favorite Foods: Tamales and fried plantains
How I Spend My Free Time: Thinking of other ways to make my poems interesting.
About Me: I am living my dream as a poet with my third wife, Matilde. Urrutia. My greatest accomplishment is winning the International Peace Prize and the Nobel Prize for Literature.

Additional Photos (28)

Personal Information
Family: Married to Matilde Urrutia
Location: Santiago, Chile
Contacts

Federico García Lorca   Jan Neruda RIP   Gabriela Mistral

Matilde Urrutia   Clifford Simak   James W. Riddleberger

Works Cited:
"Pablo "Pablo Neruda." *Poets.org*. Academy of American Poets, 2010. Web.
        4 Nov 2010. <http://www.poets.org/poet.php/prmPID/279>.
"Pablo Neruda." *Poetry Connection*. Gunnar Bengtsson, 2010. Web. 4 Nov
        2010. <http://www.poetryconnection.net/poets/Pablo_Neruda>.
"Pablo Neruda Biography." *Famous Poets and Poems.com*. 2010. Web. 4 Nov
        2010.
        <http://famouspoetsandpoems.com/poets/pablo_neruda/biography>.

TABLE 5.5 Profile Rubric

Elements	Exemplary 3	Satisfactory but lacking in some areas 2	Needs improvement 1	Score
Basic Information Content	Clear, accurate basic information is presented. Information meets the minimum requirement of these ten elements: name, gender, birthday, hometown, current residence, relationship information, education, occupation, political views, and religious views.	Some basic information is not accurate or not clearly presented. Information is missing three to five of the requirement elements. Required elements include name, gender, birthday, hometown, current residence, relationship information, education, occupation, political views, and religious views.	Basic information is incomplete, off topic, or inaccurate. Information is missing six or more of the requirement elements. Required elements include name, gender, birthday, hometown, current residence, relationship information, education, occupation, political views, and religious views.	
Personal Information Content	Clear, accurate information is presented. Information meets the minimum requirement of one of each of these ten elements: activities, interests, type of favorite music, favorite TV show, favorite movie, favorite book, favorite quotation, favorite saying, favorite food, statement about how free time is spent, and an about me statement.	Some basic information is not accurate or not clearly presented. Information is missing three to five of the requirement elements. Required elements include activities, interests, type of favorite music, favorite TV show, favorite movie, favorite book, favorite quotation, favorite saying, favorite food, statement about how free time is spent, and an about me statement.	Basic information is incomplete, off topic, or inaccurate. Information is missing six or more of the requirement elements. Required elements include activities, interests, type of favorite music, favorite TV show, favorite movie, favorite book, favorite quotation, favorite saying, favorite food, statement about how free time is spent, and an about me statement.	
Pictures	Number of pictures meets or exceeds the minimum requirement of seven pictures. Required pictures include one profile picture, three pictures in the photo album with a brief caption, and three contacts' profile pictures with names.	Two or three of the required pictures are missing. Required pictures include: one profile picture, three pictures in the photo album with a brief caption, and three contacts' profile pictures with names.	Four or more of the required pictures are missing. Required pictures include: one profile picture, three pictures in the photo album with a brief caption, and three contacts' profile pictures with names.	
Mechanics	No errors in spelling, grammar, capitalization, or punctuation. All pictures and other text sources are cited properly in MLA format on the page. Profile was uploaded to assigned classroom area.	Two or less errors in spelling, grammar, capitalization, or punctuation. All pictures and other text sources are cited, but there are some minor errors in the MLA format. Profile was uploaded to assigned classroom area.	Three or more errors in spelling, grammar, capitalization, or punctuation. No citation provided on the page. Profile was not uploaded to the assigned classroom area.	
Overall construction	Page content is original and creative. All information is filled in, page is organized, and appealing to look at.	Page content is original but lacks some creativity. Some information is missing, page is lacking some organization, and could be more appealing to look at.	Page content is not original or creative. Information is missing, page lacks organization, and is not appealing to look at.	

Total Score (out of 15)

Stage Three: Facebook Profile Page Lesson Plan

Overview

Students will be assigned or choose a poet, author, or character in a book to complete a Facebook profile page from the perspective of that person. The stage two lesson can easily be carried into a stage three lesson plan by having students complete the profile page on the Facebook website. This is a stage three lesson because unfiltered access to Facebook is required, which creates a large authentic audience for the student's products because everyone on the Internet can see it.

Information and Technology Literacy Standards

NETS3.b Students locate, organize, analyze, evaluate, synthesize, and ethically use information from a variety of sources and media.

NETS3.c Students evaluate and select information sources and digital tools based on the appropriateness to specific tasks.

NETS5.a Students advocate and practice safe, legal, and responsible use of information and technology.

NETS5.b Students exhibit a positive attitude toward using technology that supports collaboration, learning, and productivity.

NETS5.c Students demonstrate personal responsibility for lifelong learning.

NETS5.d Students exhibit leadership for digital citizenship.

NETS6.a Students understand and use technology systems.

Common Core State Standards

CC.5–8.L.3 Students use knowledge of language and its conventions when writing, speaking, reading, or listening.

CC.7.L.3.a Students choose language that expresses ideas precisely and concisely, recognizing and eliminating wordiness and redundancy.

CC.9–12.L.3 Students apply knowledge of language to understand how language functions in different contexts, to make effective choices for meaning or style, and to comprehend more fully when reading or listening.

CC.6–8.WH/SS/S/T6 Students use technology, including the Internet, to produce and publish writing and present the relationships between information and ideas clearly and efficiently.

CC.9–10.WH/SS/S/T6 Students use technology, including the Internet, to produce, publish, and update individual or shared writing products, taking advantage of technology's capacity to link to other information and to display information flexibly and dynamically.

CC.11–12.WH/SS/S/T6 Students use technology, including the Internet, to produce, publish, and update individual or shared writing products in response to ongoing feedback, including new arguments of information.

CC.7–8.W.3.a Students engage and orient the reader by establishing a context and introducing a narrator and/or characters; organize an event sequence that unfolds naturally and logically.

CC.7–8.W.3.a Students engage and orient the reader by establishing a context and point of view and introducing a narrator and/or characters; organize an event sequence that unfolds naturally and logically.

CC.9–12.W.3.a Students engage and orient the reader by setting out a problem, situation, or observation, establishing one or multiple points(s) of view, and introducing a narrator and/or characters; create a smooth progression of experiences or events.

CC.6–8.W.8 Students gather relevant information from multiple print and digital sources, using search terms effectively; assess the credibility and accuracy of each source; and quote or paraphrase the data and conclusions of others while avoiding plagiarism and following a standard format for citation.

CC.9–10.W.8 Students gather relevant information from multiple authoritative print and digital sources, using advanced searches effectively; assess the usefulness of each source in answering the research question; integrate information into the text selectively to maintain the flow of ideas, avoiding plagiarism and following a standard format for citation.

CC.11–12.W.8 Students gather relevant information from multiple authoritative print and digital sources, using advanced searches effectively; assess the strengths and limitations of each source in terms of the task, purpose, and audience; integrate information into the text selectively to maintain the flow of ideas, avoiding plagiarism and overreliance on any one source and following a standard format for citation.

CC.6.S.L.5 Students include multimedia components (e.g., graphics, image, music, sound) and visual displays in presentations to clarify information.

CC.7.S.L.5 Students include multimedia components and visual displays in presentations to clarify claims and findings and emphasize salient points.

CC.8.S.L.5 Students include multimedia components and visual displays into presentations to clarify information, strengthen claims and evidence, and add interest.

CC.9–12.S.L.5 Students make strategic use of digital media (e.g., textual, graphical, audio, visual, and interactive elements) in presentations to enhance understanding of findings, reasoning, and evidence and to add interest.

Resources Needed

Library or classroom book

Computers with Internet access

Encyclopedias, biographies, and other books to research assigned or chosen person

Technology and education Facebook pages are an excellent way to stay current on the latest gadgets, get reviews on new technologies, keep up with the latest information in the field, and network with other professionals. Here is a compiled list of Facebook pages you should check out:

American Library Association (http://www.facebook.com/alalibrary) is a Facebook page loaded with excellent information that is also disseminated through their website (http://www.ala.org) and other publications. Posts include information on conferences and other learning opportunities, author information, reviews of books and other resources, and much more.

Education Nation (http://www.facebook.com/education#!/educationnation) is a Facebook page hosted by NBC News that focuses on current education news in America.

Facebook in Education (http://www.facebook.com/education) is a Facebook page offering suggestions and examples of how educators can use Facebook in the classroom as a learning tool.

Gizmodo is a first-rate webpage for the latest news on various forms of technology and includes reviews and entertaining contests. Gizmodo's Facebook page (http://www.facebook.com/gizmodo?v=wall) has over 100,000 fans, and their overview reads, "Written by the gadget obsessed, for the gadget obsessed."

International Society for Technology in Education (http://www.facebook.com/home.php#!/pages/International-Society-for-Technology-in-Education/138122399545299) is a Facebook page dedicated to improving the use of technology in K–12 education. This nonprofit organization created the National Education Technology Standards for Students (NETS-S), National Education Technology Standards for Teachers (NETS-T), and National Education Technology Standards for Administrators (NETS-A).

LifeHacker is a technology blog that provides news and tips for using technology more efficiently. Their Facebook page (http://www.facebook.com/lifehacker?v=wall) has technology tips and helpful resources to download.

Networking Media Used

Facebook (http://www.facebook.com)

Videos on YouTube (http://www.youtube.com) or Common Craft (http://www.commoncraft.com) to view an introduction to the lesson

Creative Commons (http://search.creativecommons.org) website to find images to use

Procedures

Students will be assigned or choose a poet, author, or character in a book to create a profile page on that person. This lesson requires the teacher and/or librarian to introduce social networking websites, such as Facebook and Myspace, to the students. A discussion should take place to see how familiar students are with social networking sites. To begin the lesson, the Common Craft website offers a good introduction to what social networking is in the video *Social Networking in Plain English* (http://commoncraft.com/video-social-networking). The librarian should show appropriate examples from Facebook that could serve as an accurate model for their profile page. Students will need to learn some of the jargon that is associated with social networking sites in order to complete the assignment. Students will need to understand the following terminology: profile, status updates, wall, and friends.

Students will use the Internet and library books to research their assigned or chosen person to find the following information to complete the profile page: name, relationship status, current city, hometown, sex, birthday, an about me statement, employer, college/university, high school, religion, and political views. Students will also research the person's interest and hobbies in order to draw conclusions about personal information, such as the following: inspirational people; favorite quotations, music, books, movies, television, games, sports, teams, and athletes; activities; and interests.

Students will need to register for Facebook and friend the other members of the class (note If students already have a Facebook account they will need to sign up for another email account). Students will need to mark their profile page's privacy settings as accessible by everyone. All students will share their real name and username with the teacher for identification purposes. The teacher and librarian will also friend all the students in the class. Students will search the Creative Commons (http://search.creativecommons.org) website to find images to use on the template for the profile picture, additional pictures, and pictures of friends. Students should have one profile picture, additional pictures, names and pictures of six friends, and at least two status updates. In addition to posting their profile, each student must read at least two other students' profiles and make at least two comments to those students (as their assigned person, of course).

TABLE 5.6 Facebook Profile Rubric

Elements	Exemplary 3	Satisfactory but lacking in some areas 2	Needs improvement 1	Score
Basic information content	Clear, accurate basic information is presented. Information meets the minimum requirement of these 12 elements (name, relationship status, current city, hometown, sex, birthday, an about me statement, employer, college/university, high school, religion, and political views).	Some basic information is not accurate or not clearly presented. Information is missing three to five of the requirement elements (name, relationship status, current city, hometown, sex, birthday, an about me statement, employer, college/university, high school, religion, and political views).	Basic information is incomplete, off topic, or inaccurate. Information is missing six or more of the requirement elements (name, relationship status, current city, hometown, sex, birthday, an about me statement, employer, college/university, high school, religion, and political views).	
Personal information content	Clear, accurate information is presented. Information meets the minimum requirement of one of each of these 12 elements (people who inspire you; favorite quotations, music, books, movies, television, games, sports you play, teams, and athletes; activities; and interests).	Some basic information is not accurate or not clearly presented. Information is missing three to five of the requirement elements (people who inspire you; favorite quotations, music, books, movies, television, games, sports you play, teams, and athletes; activities; and interests).	Basic information is incomplete, off topic, or inaccurate. Information is missing six or more of the requirement elements (people who inspire you; favorite quotations, music, books, movies, television, games, sports you play, teams, and athletes; activities; and interests).	
Pictures	The number of pictures meets or exceeds the minimum requirement of four pictures. Required pictures include one profile picture and three pictures in the photo album, each with a brief caption.	One or two of the required pictures are missing. Required pictures include one profile picture and three pictures in the photo album, each with a brief caption.	Three or four of the required pictures are missing. Required pictures include one profile picture and three pictures in the photo album, each with a brief caption.	
Mechanics	No errors in spelling, grammar, capitalization, or punctuation. All pictures and other text sources are cited properly in MLA format as a status post on the page. Profile is available for everyone to view on Facebook.	Two or fewer errors in spelling, grammar, capitalization, or punctuation. All pictures and other text sources are cited, but there are some minor errors in the MLA format. Profile is available for viewing on Facebook.	Three or more errors in spelling, grammar, capitalization, or punctuation. No citation provided on the page. Profile was not available for viewing on Facebook.	
Overall construction	Page content is original and creative. All information is filled in; page is organized and appealing to look at.	Page content is original but lacks some creativity. Some information is missing; page is lacking some organization and could be more appealing to look at.	Page content is not original or creative. Information is missing; page lacks organization and is not appealing to look at.	
Interaction	Added at least three classmates' characters as friends. Exceeds the number of required comments (at least two) to other classmates' profile pages.	Added one or two classmates' characters as friends. Met the number of required comments (exactly two) to other classmates' profile pages.	Did not add any classmates' characters as friends. Did not comment on classmates' profile pages.	

Total score (out of 18)

A rubric given before the project is started will keep students on track and allow students to understand how they will be graded (see the rubric provided).

Lesson Plans Adapted for Other Subjects

Use social studies, science, math, art, or mythology learning standards to have students do this exact same lesson except substitute a historian, scientist, mathematician, artist, or god/goddess from mythology for the character. Student can create their profile pages as a historian, scientist, mathematician, artist, or god/goddess from mythology whom they were assigned or chose themselves. For example, the basic information on the famous mathematician Euclid's profile page might be the following:

Gender: Male

Birthday: August 9, 322 BC

Hometown: Alexandria, Egypt

Current Residence: Megara, Greece

Relationship Status: Married

Education: University of Alexandria

Occupation: Mathematician

6

A Few Final Words

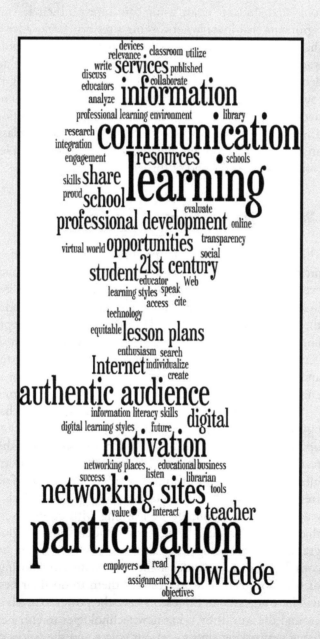

Physical libraries are the original networking places where people gather to share information and interact with others who share their passions. Today, libraries and schools exist in the virtual world, and librarians and educators must have a presence in that world. Libraries and schools, whether physical or virtual, should be free places where people can access and share information.

Like it or not, the fact remains that our students use online networking sites and enjoy spending their free time on these sites. Educators need to work with the resources that students are already using to improve students' information literacy skills to the point where they can effectively search, evaluate, utilize, and cite the abundance of information the Internet hands them. Our Web 2.0 world is based on participation, and incorporating networking sites into lesson plans ensures students are participating using the digital learning styles to which they are already accustomed.

Students can use networking sites to interact with information, build knowledge, and share that knowledge with an authentic audience. Integrating networking tools that students enjoy using can improve their learning in the classroom. Assignments that involve networking sites bring relevance to the classroom. The fact that student work will be published makes students more motivated because they want to be proud of work that is shared with others. Educators must provide students with opportunities to individualize learning or risk students' indifference toward the lesson. A large component of society does not believe in the value of networking sites and only sees these sites as a distraction to the learning process. These naysayers need to see successful examples of classroom integration if they are to become supporters. See the list of positive examples of schools utilizing networking sites at the end of this chapter.

Where We Are Now

This generation of students has grown up surrounded by digital tools. With the prevalence of Internet-accessible mobile devices (smartphones, iPads, e-readers, etc.), everyone seems to be online constantly. These students are continuously interacting in a virtual world through networking sites. Students today can get any information they want at any time. Networking sites are the way people communicate today, and libraries need to join those conversations. Libraries must show their patrons they are current by meeting their needs on their own terms. Networking sites are here to stay and will only become more important in the future for marketing library services, engaging students, and participating in professional learning environments.

Educators in the 21st century are now expected to have knowledge of technology as well as of content. Education in the 21st century should focus on the development of authentic literacy skills for students across the curriculum. Learning to read, write, listen, speak, research, critically analyze information, and communicate ideas using a variety of formats is vital for children of all ages. Some of the most frequent complaints of teachers revolve around a lack of student motivation to read, write, and communicate learning with others. Networking sites can change that common problem by increasing students' motivation to learn through the integration of a technology they already love. Not only are students more motivated to complete the project because they are excited about using the technology, but Web distribution of their work inspires them to do their best since a global audience will have access to it. Educators have the power to reach our students (and students around the world) by using new technologies to enhance learning experiences, by using networking sites to get our voices and the voices of our students heard, and by using available online resources to open up a whole new world to our students.

Incorporating networking sites into the classroom allows students to create, discuss, and collaborate while encouraging enthusiasm and engagement.

Where to Next

Using the current trends to predict the future, the forecast indicates the increase of mobile devices to access the Internet (in even smaller sizes), more equitable access for everyone as more technology is reaching rural areas, greater transparency in classrooms, and an increase in the number of people participating in social networking sites. Today's employers expect graduates to be technologically proficient and able to acquire new skills in an ever-changing world. We are severely hindering our students' future success if we ignore or limit access to networking resources. The experience students gain using networking tools for communication and collaboration will not only help them with their current learning objectives but will also be important for higher education and future employment. Most businesses today, whether large or small, use networking sites to help them promote their products and services. Employers want to hire people who already have the skills needed to promote their businesses. Most colleges are now incorporating these technologies into their classes as well as into their recruiting programs. As the lesson plans in this book demonstrate, incorporating networking technologies into the classroom is not just a fun enrichment activity, but rather is selective and intentional to teach the required standards. Networking sites offer learning opportunities that are available 24 hours a day seven days a week.

Networking Sites Used for Professional Development

School districts will face even deeper budget cuts in the near future, including cuts to professional development funds. Networking sites can help offset some of these cuts by offering a convenient, efficient, free way to enhance educators' knowledge and skills. Networking sites basically offer you customized professional development because you can learn whatever you want from experts all over the world. For teachers who spend much of their days as the only adult inside classrooms, networking sites can provide a unique platform for conversation. Using networking sites allows teachers to accomplish the following:

- Connect with other teachers for advice about classroom issues

- Gather resources for stronger classroom lesson plans

- Access cutting-edge training from across the world

- Create camaraderie between teachers from different schools (and states and countries)

The abundance of information and technological advances demands that school librarians also engage in continuing professional development to adapt to the changing needs of the learning communities they serve. Professional and personal development is vital because librarians must not only know what tasks they must perform but also how to perform those tasks to the best of their ability. We need to use every means to keep abreast of new technologies and developments, so it is time to turn to networking sites developed for librarians for professional development. In addition to learning from networking sites, we need to contribute to the global learning community by making our work public for others to learn from.

Educators Worth Checking Out

The Unquiet Library at Creekview High School in Canton, Georgia, has a presence on most networking sites. Buffy Hamilton and Roxanne Johnson are the school librarians and are recognized as leaders in the field. Their sites include the following:

The Unquiet Library Blog http://theunquietlibrary.wordpress.com/

The Unquiet Library on Facebook https://www.facebook.com/pages/The-Unquiet-Library-Creekview-High-School-Media-Center/31676317923

The Unquiet Library on Twitter http://twitter.com/#!/unquietlibrary

The Unquiet Library on FriendFeed http://friendfeed.com/theunquietlibrary

The Unquiet Library's Google Profile https://profiles.google.com/theunquietlibrary#theunquietlibrary/about

The Unquiet Library on YouTube http://www.youtube.com/user/theunquietlibrary

The Unquiet Library's Flickr Photostream http://www.flickr.com/photos/8166472@N03/

Eric Sheninger is the principal at New Milford High School in New Milford, New Jersey. Mr. Sheninger is an advocate for social networking in schools and can be found on the following sites:

New Milford High School Website http://www.newmilfordschools.org/NMHS/hs_main_page.html

New Milford High School on Twitter http://twitter.com/#!/NMHS_Principal

New Milford High School on Facebook https://www.facebook.com/pages/New-Milford-High-School/103758836330278

New Milford High School on YouTube http://www.youtube.com/user/NMHSPrincipal

Eric Sheninger's website and blog http://ericsheninger.com/esheninger

Eric Sheninger's Google Profile https://plus.google.com/112337616865529158178#112337616865529158178/posts

Vicki Davis, a.k.a. Cool Cat Teacher, is a computer science teacher at Westwood Schools. Westwood Schools is a private college preparatory school for grades K through 12 located in Camilla, Georgia. Ms. Davis is a teacher, cofounder of the Flat Classroom Project, blogger, and presenter. Some of her sites include the following:

Cool Cat Teacher's blog http://coolcatteacher.blogspot.com

Cool Cat Teacher on Twitter http://twitter.com/coolcatteacher

Cool Cat Teacher on Facebook http://www.facebook.com/pages/Cool-Cat-Teacher/143588425657314?sk = wall&filter = 12

Cool Cat Teacher on LinkedIn http://www.linkedin.com/in/coolcatteacher

Cool Cat Teacher on YouTube http://www.youtube.com/user/coolcatteacher

Cool Cat Teacher's Flickr Photostream http://www.flickr.com/photos/48764499@N00

Cool Cat Teacher on Blip.tv http://blip.tv/coolcatteacher

References

American Library Association. 2010. "AASL Votes to Adopt the Professional Title School Librarian." http://www.ala.org/ala/newspresscenter/news/pressreleases2010/january2010/adopt_aasl.cfm (accessed June 12, 2011).

Bill and Melinda Gates Foundation. 2006. "The Silent Epidemic: Perspectives on High School Dropouts." http://www.gatesfoundation.org/united-states/Documents/TheSilentEpidemic-ExecSum.pdf (accessed June 12, 2011).

Child Molestation Research and Prevention Institute. 2011. "Tell Others the Facts." http://www.childmolestationprevention.org/pages/tell_others_the_facts.html (accessed July 10, 2011).

Electronic Privacy Information Center. 2011. "Family Educational Rights and Privacy Act." http://epic.org/privacy/education/ferpa.html (accessed June 12, 2011).

Empowering Learners: Guidelines for School Library Media Programs. 2009. Chicago: American Library Association.

Federal Trade Commission. 2010. "Children's Online Privacy Protection Act of 1998." http://www.ftc.gov/ogc/coppa1.htm (accessed June 12, 2011).

Information Power: Guidelines for School Library Media Programs. 1988. Chicago: American Library Association.

International Society for Technology in Education. 2007. "National Educational Technology Standards for Students."http://www.iste.org/standards/nets-for-students/nets-student-standards-2007.aspx (accessed June 9, 2011).

Internet Free Expression Alliance. 2001. "Children's Internet Protection Act." http://ifea.net/cipa.pdf (accessed June 12, 2011).

Ipsos.com. 2011. "One Quarter (27%) Of American Teens Use Facebook Continuously Throughout the Day," http://www.ipsos-na.com/news-polls/pressrelease.aspx?id=5095 (accessed June 12, 2011).

Lehr, Camilla, et al. 2004. *Essential Tools: Increasing Rates of School Completion.* Minneapolis, MN: National Center on Secondary Education and Transition.

Lenhart, Amanda, Kristen Purcell, Aaron Smith, and Kathryn Zickuhur. 2010. "Social Media and Mobile Internet Use Among Teens and Young Adults." http://www.pewinternet.org/~/media//Files/Reports/2010/PIP_Social_Media_and_Young_Adults_Report_Final_with_toplines.pdf (accessed July 10, 2011).

McGinnis, John. 2002. "The Names We Call Ourselves—Redux." *CSLA Journal* 26 (1): 8–9.

National Governors Association Center for Best Practices and Council of Chief State School Officers. 2011. "Common Core State Standards for English Language Arts & Literacy in History/Social Studies, Science, and Technical Subjects." http://www.corestandards.org/assets/CCSSI_ELA%20 Standards.pdf (accessed June 9, 2011).

White House. 2010. "President Obama Announces Steps to Reduce Dropout Rate and Prepare Students for College and Careers." http://www.whitehouse.gov/the-press-office/president-obama-announces-steps-reduce-dropout-rate-and-prepare-students-college-an (accessed August 10, 2011).

Appendix

INSTRUCTIONS FOR SETTING UP A YOUTUBE ACCOUNT AND UPLOADING VIDEOS

Images used with permission from Google, YouTube brand owner (http://www.youtube.com/). All rights reserved.

This handout can be used to set up your own account (also known as a video channel), upload videos into that account, and subscribe to someone else's video channel.

1. To begin the account setup process, go to http://www.youtube.com and then click on the "Create Account" link in the top-right corner to continue to the YouTube Account Application Form.

Most of the application form is just standard details for you to fill out—email address, location, postal code, date of birth, and gender. The second and most important field in the application form is the "username," otherwise known as your "account name" or your "video channel name." Remember, this is the name everyone sees next to the videos you post, so keep it professional and as descriptive of your library as possible. Only letters and numbers are allowed in the username, so do not use spaces or special characters. Type the username you would like to use and click on the "Check Availability"

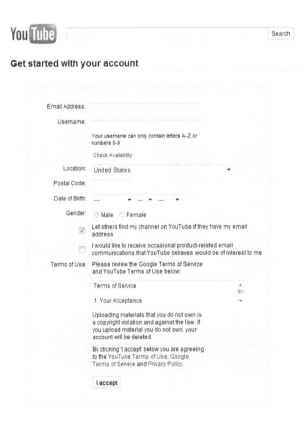

From *The Networked Library: A Guide for the Educational Use of Social Networking Sites* by Melissa A. Purcell. Santa Barbara, CA: Linworth. Copyright © 2012.

link. Once you find a username that is available and you have filled in the rest of the application form, click on the "I Accept" button after reading the "Terms of Use" to continue.

Signing up for YouTube means creating a Google account that you can use to access YouTube, iGoogle, Picasa, and many other Google services. After clicking on the "I Accept" button, you are then asked if you would like this new YouTube ac-

count attached to your existing Google account. If you have an existing Google account, all you have to do is enter your existing Google account password and hit the "Link Accounts" button. Skip to Step 2 once you have linked your accounts.

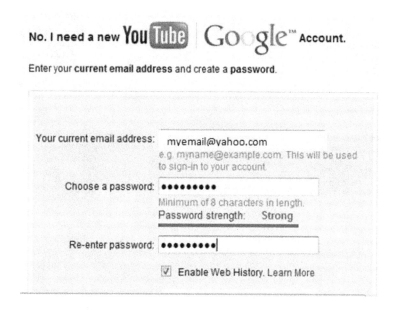

If you do not have an existing Google account, you can create one by entering your current email address and creating a password that is a minimum of eight characters in length.

When you have filled in this easy Google account application form, the word verification box will appear to let Google/YouTube know that a human is applying for the Google account rather than a malicious piece of software. Your new Google account will automatically be attached to your new YouTube account once you click on the "Create New Account and Finish" button to continue.

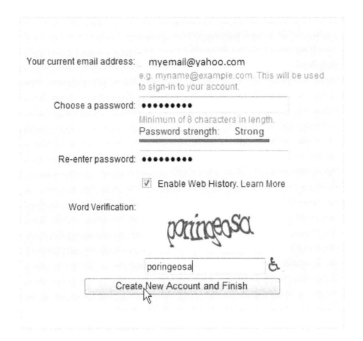

After clicking on the "Create New Account and Finish" button, the following success message will appear, asking you to check your email in order to verify ownership of the email address you supplied in the Google account application form. So the next thing you should do is close this window, as it will not be needed again, and then go and check your email from the supplied email address.

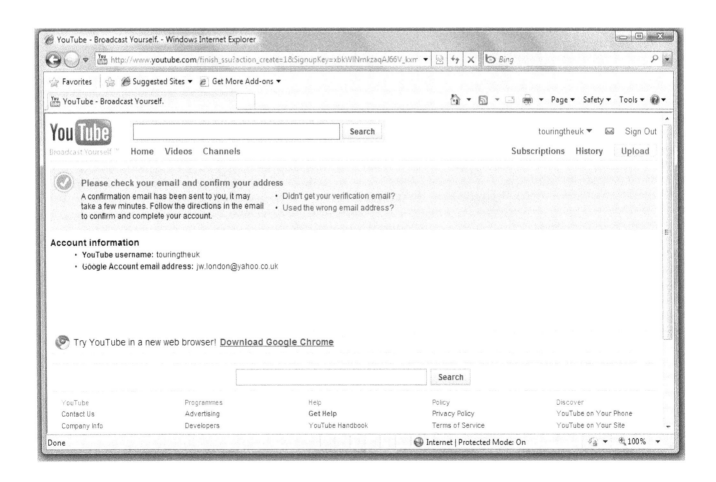

The email message in your inbox should look similar to the following. Click on the "Email Verification" link to verify the email address for your new Google/YouTube account.

Welcome to Google Accounts. To activate your account and verify your email address, please click the following link:

https://www.google.com/accounts/VE?service=youtube&c=COH0z8Ws=en

NOTE Please print this page for your records. You'll need your verification link if you lose access to your account (for example, if you forget your username or password).

If you've received this mail in error, it's likely that another user entered your email address while trying to create an account for a different email address. If you don't click the verification link, the account won't be activated.

If you didn't request this email, but you decide to use this account, or delete it, you'll first need to reset the account password by entering your email address at https://www.google.com/accounts/recovery?service=youtube&continuewww.youtube.

If clicking the link above does not work, copy and paste the URL in a new browser window instead.

Thank you for using Google.

For questions or concerns about your account, please visit the Google Accounts Help Center at http://www.google.com/support/accounts/

This is a post-only mailing. Replies to this message are not monitored or answered.

When your supplied email address has been verified, a new Web browser window will open to display the YouTube website where you can sign in.

2. Once you are signed into your new YouTube account, you are ready to upload your first video, so click the "Upload" (next to "Browse") button at the top of the website.

You will be taken to a new screen where you can hit the "Upload Video" button on this screen to select your file to upload.

Video File Upload

Upload video or Record from webcam	**Videos can be...** • High Definition • Up to 2 GB in size. • Up to 15 minutes in length. • A wide variety of formats

You will have to navigate to where you have saved the video that you want to upload. Select the video and hit the "Open" button to continue.

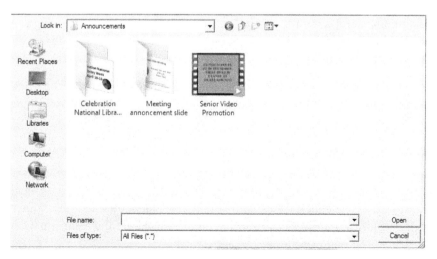

As soon as you have selected the video you want to upload, YouTube begins processing your selected video file. Processing could take several minutes depending on the length of your video. Note: sometimes video files are not accepted by YouTube. YouTube accepts the following file types/formats and the length of videos, so try to use .wmv, .flv, .mov, .avi, or .mpg videos with mp3 audio where possible, and try to keep the display size (resolution) down to 640 x 480.

Video File Upload

🎞 **Senior Video Promotion.wmv** (9.94M)

Upload progress:	████████████	77%	cancel

Less than a minute remaining...

Preview:

Video information and privacy settings ⊗

Title: Senior Video Promotion.wmv

Description:

Tags:

Category: -- Select a category -- ▼

Privacy: ⦿ Public (anyone can search for and view - recommended)

◯ Unlisted (anyone with the link can view) Learn more

◯ Private (only specific YouTube users can view)

Save changes or Skip for now

Sharing options

URL:

Embed:

While your video file is being uploaded, you can enter a title, description, and some tags (keywords) to help viewers search for your video and understand what it is about. The tags should contain high-ranking words that best describe your video content and, more importantly, words that a viewer is likely to use in order to search for your video in the first place (such as the name of your library).

After entering the title, description, and tags you then need to select a category, from the category drop-down menu, for your video. The Education category is often a good choice for many library videos that you would upload. Once that is done, you then need to decide whether or not to make your video public (everyone can search for and view your video), unlisted (only people with the link can access the video), or private (account log-in is required to view) by selecting the appropriate "Share" or "Private" setting. When you have decided which option to use, click on the "Save Changes" button to continue. Remember, if you are posting videos to increase public relations then you will want as many viewers as you can get, so you will want to make sure your videos are marked "Public." *It is important to ensure that any videos you create adhere to current copyright guidelines.* If someone likes your video(s), they may subscribe to your channel so that anytime you upload more videos they are automatically informed. You can do the same—just click on the "Subscribe" button when you see a video, or collection of videos, you like.

INSTRUCTIONS TO CUSTOMIZE YOUR YOUTUBE CHANNEL

Once you have set up an account on YouTube, your channel has been created (note that on YouTube the word *account* is synonymous with *channel,* so once you have set up your account your channel is set up). You should customize your channel to fit your school or content. YouTube has lots of options to change the look of your channel, but I recommend at least the following five options:

1. Select a Color Scheme Using Your School Colors or the Primary Colors Used in Your Library

When you are logged in, click on your logon name in the upper right-hand corner. Then select "My Channel" from the drop-down menu.

Once your channel appears, select the "Themes and Colors" tab. Then select the "Show Advanced Options" button at the bottom.

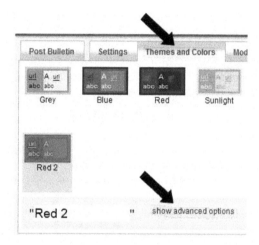

You can select colors by hitting the thumbnail next to the option or by entering the corresponding hex triplet (which can be found online on several sites such as http://en.wikipedia.org/wiki/Web_colors). Make sure you pay special attention to the color of the text to ensure it is legible. Click the "Save Changes" button at the bottom.

2. Create a Custom Background Using Your School Mascot or Library Logo

Generally, most schools and libraries already have customized images that are used on websites, newsletters, and so forth that can be uploaded to YouTube in a few short steps. If you do not already have a logo or mascot image created, then you might have to create one yourself or find someone to create one for you. Some things to keep in mind: the picture cannot exceed 256 kilobytes and will look best at 1,500 pixels wide and 2,000 pixels tall.

To add your own image, follow the same steps as in step 1 (Click on your YouTube username at the top right of your screen and select "My Channel." Next, select "Themes and Colors." Then click on "Show Advanced Options" for the ability to upload your new background image). Select the "Browse" button to find the picture you want to upload. You have the option of having only one image or having the image repeat multiple times (check the "Repeat Background" box at the bottom of the page if you want this option) as your background. Click the "Save Changes" button at the bottom.

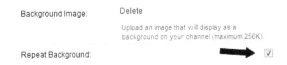

3. Make Your Best Video the "Featured" Video to Ensure Everyone Sees it First

By default, YouTube shows your most recent video in the main "Featured" window on your channel page. While this may be ideal for YouTubers who post regular content and do not really care which one is viewed first, as a library channel the featured video should be one that highlights the best of your program.

To change your channel's "Featured" clip, go to your "My Channel" settings and select the "Video and Playlists" tab at the top. The last dropdown is the "Featured Video" menu; you can choose a video from the list or, by selecting "other," you can also paste the URL of the video you want to feature. You can check the box to autoplay the video whenever someone goes onto your channel. Click the "Save Changes" button at the bottom.

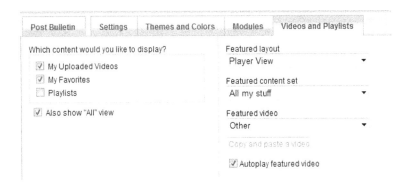

4. Make Sure All Your Thumbnails Have a Still Picture That Represents the Video

When you select your video to view, you will see a list of menu options at the top. Select the "Edit Video Detail" box on the far left side.

Next select "Video Thumbnail" from the options that pop up.

You will be given three options of thumbnails to choose from, so select the one that best represents the video. Click the "Save Changes" button at the bottom.

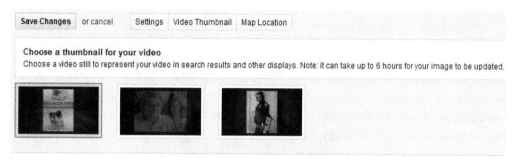

5. Add Channel Tags to Make Your Channel Easy to Find

The way for people to find your content is through your tags. You need to take the time to tag your channel with relevant key words just as you did when you uploaded your videos. I recommend tagging your school or library name, your city and state, the word *library*, and anything else that applies to your program.

To add tags, go to the "My Channel" menu and select "Settings."

INSTRUCTIONS FOR SETTING UP A GLOGSTER EDU ACCOUNT

1. Go to http://edu.glogster.com.

2. Click on the "Sign Up" button in the upper right of the screen.

3. You are given a choice of several accounts. Choose the free "Basic Teacher" account on the right side by clicking the "Get It" button.

4. Fill out the general online registration form with your nickname (the same thing as screen name or login), password, email, first name, last name, birthday, gender, country, state (once you select your state, the city, district, and school drop boxes will appear). Make sure you check that you accept the "Terms of Use" and type in the randomly generated code to verify that you are human. Click the "Sign Up" button.

5. You will need to check the email account you provided for a confirmation email from glogster.com. When you receive the email, click the "Confirm Your Account by Clicking Here" link in the email.

6. Once you are logged into your account, you can set up student accounts on your "Dashboard" by selecting the "Add New Students" option in the middle of the page.

On the next screen, enter the number of students you want to add (up to 200 students). Glogster will assign random nicknames and passwords (the students can change the password later and enter their first and last name for easy identification), or you can upload an excel document with this information (nickname, first and last name, and password).

Add new students to your class

How many accounts do you want to add? 199   Still 199 unused accounts.

ADD ACCOUNTS

Or download and fill out a file in the Excel Format (it's easier).
The Excel tool is available only under PC platform and it is Excel file for Microsoft Office 2007 & 2003!
If you are using older version of MS Excel, please download the following plugin from Microsoft page and install it first.

DOWNLOAD FILE

Video tutorial of using Excel import tool:
http://glogsteredu.edu.glogster.com/excel-import-tool/

For 200 student accounts purchase EDU Premium.

INSTRUCTIONS FOR STUDENT GLOGSTER EDU ACCOUNT SETUP

Images used with permission from Glogster EDU (http://edu.glogster.com). All rights reserved.

1. Go to http://edu.glogster.com.

2. Click on the "Log In" button in the upper right corner of the page. Use the nickname and password provided by your teacher.

3. Once you are logged into your account, click on the "Edit My Profile" button at the top of the page.

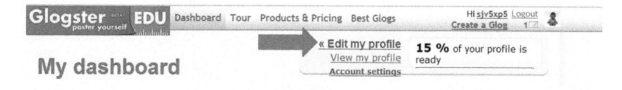

4. When the "Edit My Profile" box opens, type your first and last name in the text box (if it is not already provided). Also type a new password that you can easily remember in the text box.

Tell us something about yourself sj 5xp5

Edit your name so your teacher and classmates can identify you more easily. Note: Your name will only be visible to your registered teacher and classmates.

First name: ASample

Last name: Student

Gender: ○ male ◉ female

Forget Blogging, try Glogging!

To Create Teacher Accounts

1. Go to http://animoto.com/education.

2. Click on the "Sign Up" button at the top of the screen.

3. Fill out the general online registration form—email, password, first name, last name, birthday, and gender. Click the "Sign Up" button.

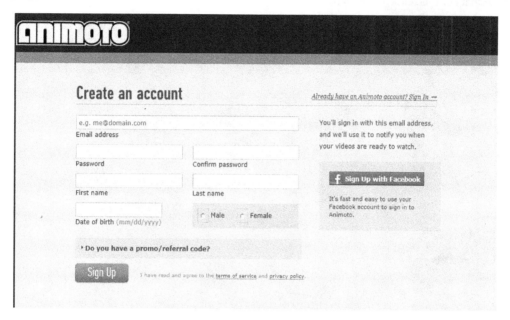

4. Fill out the education application—first and last name, school name, grades you teach, subjects you teach, your school email address, and your class website/blog (this is optional). Click the "Submit Application" button. Note that applications can take several weeks to be approved, so planning ahead is essential.

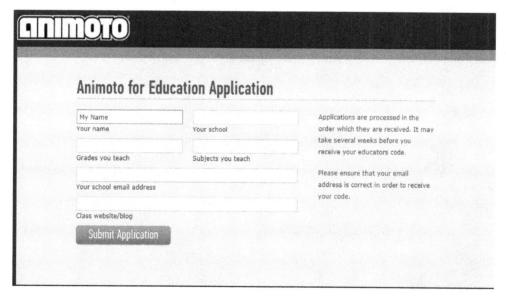

5. You will need to check the email account you provided for a confirmation email with the education promotion codes that you will need to provide to your students.

To Create Student Accounts

1. Go to http://animoto.com/education.

2. Click on the "Sign Up" button at the top of the screen.

3. Fill out the general online registration form—email, password, first name, last name, birthday, and gender. Click the arrow next to the question "Do you have a promo/referral code?" Type the educational promotion code provided by your teacher in the box that appears. Click the "Sign Up" button.

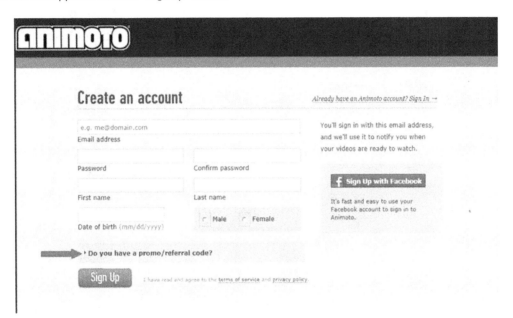

INSTRUCTIONS FOR CREATING A VIDEO IN ANIMOTO

1. Find Creative Commons licensed videos and images that relate to your assigned topic. Save them all in one folder. Remember, you will need a slide citing your information and video/image sources, so it is best to type that information into a PowerPoint slide and then save that slide as an image file in your same folder.

2. Log into your Animoto account at http://animoto.com/education.

3. Click the "Create Video" button in the top right corner.

4. Choose a video style by clicking the "Create" button underneath your chosen style. Only chose a style that states "Create" underneath it or you will be asked to pay an additional fee to upgrade.

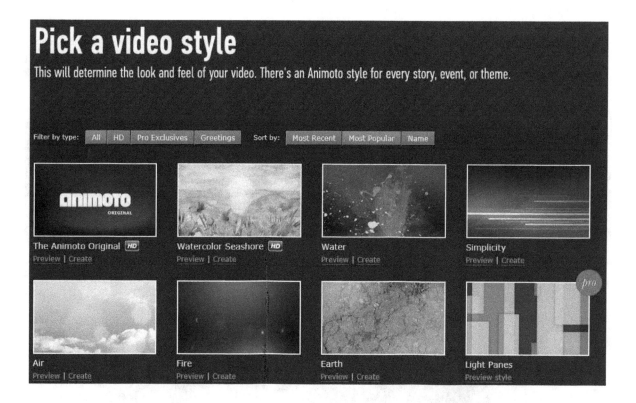

5. Upload all of your saved videos and images (using Ctrl + A to select all the files in your saved folder) to your video.

6. Your images should appear in boxes. Underneath these boxes, there are icons for "add more," "add text," "spotlight," etc. Select the "add text" button on the bottom to add text. You are limited to 52 characters, so write concisely. You may divide the text between two slides, if needed. You can move the boxes around to arrange your film. Hit "Done" when finished.

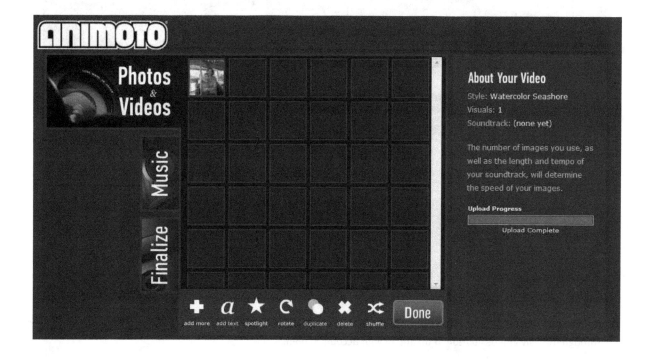

7. Add music to your film—either Animoto's selection or your own—by selecting the "Music" tab on the left. Once you have uploaded your own music or clicked the "Select" button next to the song title in Animoto's music list, click the "Continue" button at the bottom. On the next screen, keep the speed the same by clicking the "Continue" button at the bottom.

8. Title your video and make sure your name is included in the provided box. Click the "Create Video" button at the bottom.

9. Animoto will email you when your video is finished. You can always edit the film (change the song, images, speed, etc.) through the "My Videos" button at the top of your account screen.

 From *The Networked Library: A Guide for the Educational Use of Sites* by Melissa A. Purcell. Santa Barbara, CA: Linworth. Copyright © 2012

INSTRUCTIONS FOR SETTING UP A ONE TRUE MEDIA ACCOUNT

This work is licensed under a Creative Commons Attribution-Sharealike 3.0 Unported License. Melissa Purcell, Owner/Creator.

1. Go to http://www.onetruemedia.com.

2. Click on the "Register" button at the top of the screen.

3. Fill out the general online registration form—email, first name, password—and agree to the "Terms of Use." Click the "Join Now" button.

INSTRUCTIONS FOR CREATING A VIDEO USING ONE TRUE MEDIA

This work is licensed under a Creative Commons Attribution-Sharealike 3.0 Unported License. Melissa Purcell, Owner/Creator.

1. Find Creative Commons licensed videos and images that relate to your assigned topic. Save them all in one folder. Remember, you will need a slide citing your information and video/image sources, so it is best to type that information into a PowerPoint slide and then save that slide as an image file in your same folder.

2. Log into your One True Media account at http://www.onetruemedia.com.

3. Click the "Create" tab at the top of the page. Click the "Get Started" button in the middle of the page.

4. Click the "Select Files" button.

5. Upload all of your saved videos and images (using Ctrl + A to select all the files in your saved folder) to the video you are creating. All the files you selected are now queued, so you must select them all (using Ctrl + A) and click the "Upload" button.

6. Click on "Done" when the pictures are uploaded. Press the "Edit" tab at the top. This is where you can change the order of the pictures or videos, the image motion, how long a particular picture will be shown, and transitions. There are little numbers at the bottom of each picture stating their order. Click on these number and type the new number order you would like. Clicking on the center of a picture will take you to the screen where you can change the image motion, how long that particular picture will be viewed, and the way it will transition to the next picture. Just use the drop-down menus. Use the green arrows to move back and forth among the pictures. Click on "Update" at the top right after you make any changes.

7. Click on the "Music" tab at the top. A playlist will come up. You can either upload your own music already saved in your music file or choose one of theirs. Click "Add" next to a song in the One True Media playlist to add it to your video or upload your own song.

8. Once your music is added, your video is complete. You can go to the "My Videos" tab at the top to share your video through Facebook, YouTube, Twitter or email or embed it on your blog.

INSTRUCTIONS FOR CREATING A VIDEO USING JAYCUT

1. Find Creative Commons licensed videos, images, and audio files that relate to your assigned topic. Save them all in one folder. Remember, you will need a slide citing your information and video/image sources, so it is best to type that information into a PowerPoint slide and then save that slide as an image file in your same folder.

2. Log into your JayCut account at http://jaycut.com.

3. Click the "Create Movie" button in the middle of the page.

4. Click the "Add Media" button on the far right side of the screen.

5. On the next screen, choose "My Computer" as the source of the media, and then click the "Next" button.

6. Click the "Browse" button to search for the folder with your saved videos, images, and audio files.

7. Upload all of your saved videos, images, and audio files (using Ctrl + A to select all the files in your saved folder). All the files you selected are now showing, but you must click the "Upload" button.

8. Click on the "Video," "Images," or "Audio" tabs at the top to view the media that you just uploaded. All of your media are listed under those tabs and need to be dragged down to the movie timeline in the position that you want them.

9. Click on the "Text" tab at the top. Type in any text slides that you want to add to your movie.

10. Once you have your video timeline the way you want it, you need to click the "Publish/Download Movie" button in the bottom right corner of the screen. Select "Computer" as the place you want to publish your movie. Click the "Next" button.

11. Select "MPEG-4" as the way you would like to publish your movie. Click the "Next" button.

12. Enter the email address that you want JayCut to send the link of your saved video to.

INSTRUCTIONS FOR SEARCHING FOR CREATIVE COMMONS LICENSED VIDEOS, IMAGES, AND AUDIO

Images licensed under a HYPERLINK "http://creativecommons.org/licenses/by/3.0/" Creative Commons Attribution license by Creative Commons (http://creativecommons.org).

1. Go to http://search.creativecommons.org.

2. Type in your keywords/phrases in the search box. Make sure the "Modify, Adapt, or Build Upon" box is checked, but you can *uncheck* the "Use for Commercial Purposes" box.

3. Select which site you would like to search by clicking on "Google" (to search the Web for images, videos, and audio), "Google Image" (for images), "Flickr" (for images), "Blip.tv" (for videos), "Jamendo" (for music), "SpinXpress" (for images, videos, and audio), or "Wikimedia Commons" (for images, videos, and audio).

4. Once you find the media you would like to use in the results list, right-click on it and "Open Link in a New Window." This takes you to the actual website that the file can be found on so that you can record your citation information. You will need to check the Creative Commons license on this page. There are six main Creative Commons licenses; here is a general overview of all six in order from least restrictive to most restrictive:

   Attribution is the least restrictive of the licenses because it allows others to distribute, display, perform, remix, tweak, and use any derivative works based upon it, even commercially, as long as they credit you for the original creation.

   Attribution-ShareAlike is a license that allows others to distribute, display, perform, remix, tweak, and use any derivative works based upon it, even commercially, as long as they credit you for the original creation and license their new creations under the identical terms (thus any derivatives will also allow commercial use).

   Attribution-NoDerivs is a license that allows others to download, copy, display, and distribute your works, commercial and noncommercial, as long as they give credit to you and they do not change them in any way.

   Attribution-NonCommercial is a license that allows others to distribute, display, perform, remix, tweak, and use any derivative works based upon it, *except* commercially, as long as they credit you for the original creation.

   Attribution-NonCommercial-ShareAlike is a license that allows others to distribute, display, perform, remix, tweak, and use any derivative works based upon it, *except* commercially, as long as they credit you for the original creation *and* license their new creations under the identical terms (thus any derivatives will also prohibit commercial use).

   Attribution-NonCommercial-NoDerivs is the most restrictive of licenses, only allowing others to download, copy, display, and distribute your works as long as they give credit to you and they do not change them in any way or use them commercially.

5. Create a citation for your Creative Commons file following this format:

   "[File Title]." [Website Name]. Web. [Date Accessed]. [URL]

   Example:

   "Baby Toes." Flickr. Web. 14 Nov 2011. http://www.flickr.com/photos/40765798@N00/2396559684/

INSTRUCTIONS LETTER FOR PATRONS TO SET UP A TWITTER ACCOUNT

Dear Patron,

This year, the staff at _____ library will be using Twitter (http://twitter.com) to keep you up-to-date with the newest information immediately as it is happening. If you are not already a member of Twitter and would like us to walk you through the sign-up process, just stop by and see us. As always, we are here to help and would *love* to see you!

If you are not familiar with Twitter, here is the basic information: Twitter is a free website that allows people to communicate through concise statements consisting of 140 characters or less.

The library staff invites you to sign up to follow our Twitter account using the directions here. Once you have signed up to follow us, you will receive our messages instantly on your Twitter page and can sign up to receive these messages on your cell phone (please note: standard text rates apply).

The steps for signing up for a Twitter account and following us are as follows:

1. In order to open a Twitter account, you must have an email address. If you do not have your own email address, you can create a free one with Gmail (http://www.gmail.com) or Yahoo (http://www.yahoo.com). As soon as you have an email address, proceed to step 2.

2. Go to http://twitter.com.

3. On the right side of the page you will see the statement "New to Twitter? Join Today!" Fill in the appropriate textboxes with your full name and email and choose a password to use. Then hit the "Sign Up" button.

4. Once you are logged into your new Twitter account, type in our library username, which is _____, in the top search box.

5. Once you see our account, you will see a "+ Follow" button. Click that button—You are now following us.

If you do not want to sign up to follow us, you can still view the information by going to the site at http://twitter.com/_____. You should either bookmark the site or add it to your favorites list so that you can visit it often because there are new postings daily.

INSTRUCTIONS FOR CREATING A WORD CLOUD USING WORDLE

1. Go to http://www.wordle.net.

2. Click the "Create" tab at the top.

3. Type your text in a Word document and cut and paste that information into the provided box. Click the "Go" button.

   Tip: To keep phrases together use a ~ (tilde) between words such as "High~School~Librarian"

   Tip: Ctrl + A to select all, Ctrl + C to copy, and Ctrl + V to paste.

4. After a few seconds, the word cloud appears. The "Language" button will allow you to check your spelling, remove numbers, remove foreign words, and change the case; the "Layout" button will allow you to change the word cloud shape; and the "Color" button will allow you to change the color pattern. The "Randomize" button will recreate the word cloud in a different way.

   Tips: Right clicking on a word allows you to delete that word from your word cloud.

5. Once the word cloud appears the way you would like it, click the "Print" button, then select.pdf. This will allow you to save it to your desktop. An alternate to this saving option is to hold the Ctrl + Print Screen buttons while you have your Wordle on the screen, and then you can paste (Ctrl + V or right click, "Paste") into a Word document.

INSTRUCTIONS FOR CREATING A WORD CLOUD USING TAGXEDO

1. Go to http://www.tagxedo.com.

2. Click the "Create" tab at the top.

3. Type your text in a Word document and cut and paste that information into the provided box *or* upload the saved document by clicking the "Browse" button. Click the "Submit" button.

   Tip: To keep phrases together use a ~ (tilde) between words such as "High~School~Librarian"

   Tip: Ctrl + A to select all, Ctrl + C to copy, and Ctrl + V to paste.

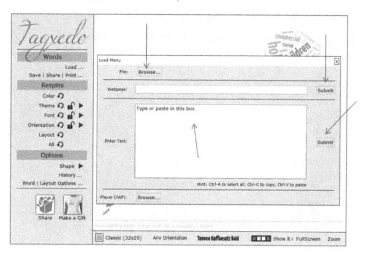

4. After a few seconds the word cloud appears. The "Respins" menu allows you to change the color, theme, font, orientation, and layout. The "Options" menu allows you to change the shape.

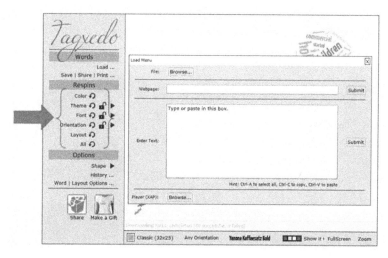

5. Once the word cloud appears the way you would like it, click the "Save," "Share," or "Print" buttons at the top.

Teacher Account Signup

1. Go to https://my.pbworks.com/?p = create.

2. In the middle of the screen you will see the message "Create a PBworks Account." Under that message, fill in the registration form with your name, email address, and chosen password. Then click the "Create Account" button.

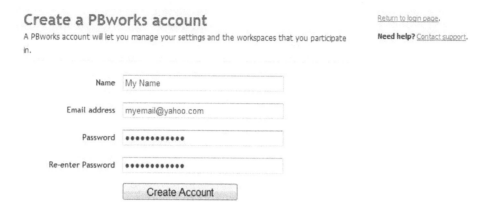

3. You will have to verify your account by following the link in an email (from PBworks Registration) sent to the email address you provided.

Create a New Workspace

Once you are able to log in to your new account, you will be able to create a workspace.

1. When logged in to http://my.pbworks.com, click the "Create a New Workspace" button in the lower right corner.

2. On the next screen you will need to give your site a name (only letters and numbers are allowed). This will be part of the URL for your site on the Internet—your workspace address will be http://XXXXXXXX.pbworks.com, where XXXXXXXX is the workspace name you chose. On this screen, you will also need to check the box for education and agree that this site will not be used for commercial purposes. The last step on this screen is to click the "Next" button.

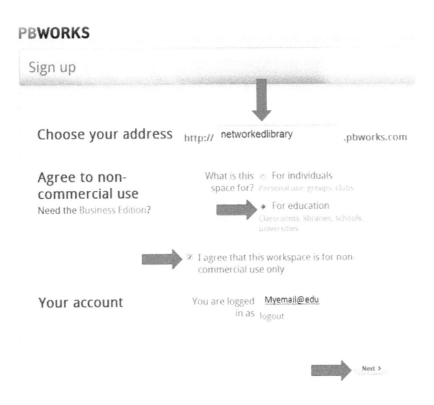

3. The final step determines who can view your site. You can either allow "Anyone" (meaning your wiki is public for anyone to search for and view) or "Only People I Invite or Approve" (meaning your wiki is private but you can allow specific people to view it). Finally, you will have to check the box to agree to the terms of service and click the "Take Me to My Workspace" button to complete the set up.

Teacher Account Signup

1. Go to http://www.wikispaces.com/content/for/teachers.

2. In the middle of the screen you will see the message "Create Your Free K–12 Wiki." Under that message, fill in the registration form with a chosen username, chosen password, and email address. Check "Yes" to the question "Do you want to create a wiki?" You will need to give your site a name (only letters and numbers are allowed). This will be part of the URL for your site on the Internet—your workspace address will be http://XXXXXXXX. wikispaces.com, where XXXXXXXX is the workspace name you chose. Check the box that you want a free private education account. Check the box to verify that you will be using the wiki for K–12 education purposes and click the "Join" button.

3. You may have to verify your account by following the link in an email sent to the address you provided.

To Create Student Accounts

Once you have logged into your new wiki, you can create up to 100 free student accounts at one time by following these steps:

1. Select "Manage Wiki" from the toolbar.

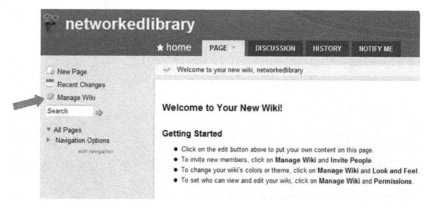

2. Under "People," select "User Creator."

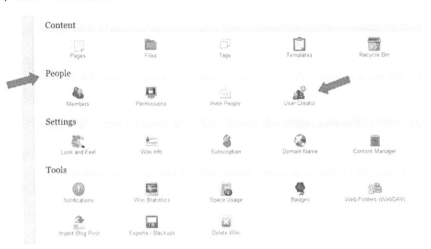

3. Choose the wiki you would like to add the users to. Also choose how you would like to enter your list—either "I will upload a spreadsheet file from my computer (.csv,.xls, or.xlsx)" or "I will paste in a text list (comma-separated or tab-separated)." Upload or paste your file with usernames, passwords, and email addresses. Email addresses and passwords are not required to create accounts but make keeping up with log-on information easier. Keep in mind that every Wikispaces username must be unique. Try using numbers, or initials, or a first name–last name combination to create unique usernames. Click the "Continue" button and your student accounts are created.

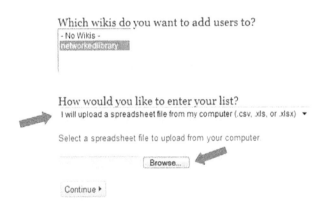

or

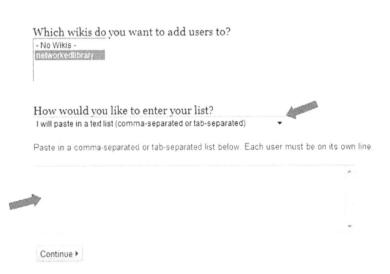

Instructions for Creating a Podcast Using Vocaroo

1. Go to http://vocaroo.com.

2. Connect your microphone. When the Adobe Flash Player Settings box appears, click the "Allow" button to allow Vocaroo access to your microphone and/or camera.

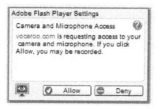

3. Click the "Click to Record" button in the center of the screen to begin recording.

4. Click the "Click to Stop" button in the center of the screen to end recording.

5. The finished recording can be listened to and recorded again, if needed. There are four options for saving: send the link in an email, post on the Internet, download as a WAV file, or download as an Ogg file.

Vocaroo - The premier voice recording service.

Record Again

Listen

Send to a friend >>

Post on the internet >>

Download as WAV - Download as Ogg

INSTRUCTIONS FOR CREATING A VOKI AND EMBEDDING ON A WIKI

1. Go to http://www.voki.com/create.php.

2. Click on the "Customize Your Character" box to choose your character, his or her clothes, and his or her bling (accessories). Click the "Done" button when you have finished customizing your character.

3. In the "Give It A Voice" box, select how you would like to provide the text to be read by your Voki—record by phone, type the text, record with a microphone, or upload an audio file. Click the "Done" button when you have added your audio.

4. In the "Backgrounds" box, you can select the background for your Voki. Click the "Done" button when you have selected your background.

5. In the "Players" box, you can select the color for the player that appears around your Voki. Click the "Done" button when you have selected your player.

6. Click the "Publish" button at the bottom. Type a title for your Voki. The next screen allows you to copy and paste the code needed to embed your Voki on a wiki or other website.

INSTRUCTIONS LETTER FOR PATRONS TO SET UP A FACEBOOK ACCOUNT

Dear Patron,

This year, the staff at _____ library will be using Facebook (http://facebook.com) to keep you up-to-date with important information, get feedback from you, and provide you with more information on our resources and services. If you are not already a member of Facebook and would like us to walk you through the sign-up process, just stop by and see us. As always, we are here to help and would *love* to see you!

If you are not familiar with Facebook, here is the basic information: Facebook is a free social networking website that allows people to communicate by posting comments on other users' walls, through personal email, and by posting videos and pictures.

The library staff invites you to sign up to "friend" us on Facebook using the directions here. Once you are friends with us, you will receive our messages instantly on your news feed.

The steps for signing up for a Facebook account and becoming our friend are as follows:

1. In order to open a Facebook account you must have an email address. If you do not have your own email address, you can create a free one with Gmail (http://www.gmail.com) or Yahoo (http://www.yahoo.com). As soon as you have an email address, proceed to step 2.

2. Go to http://facebook.com.

3. On the right side of the page you will see the statement "Sign Up." Fill in the appropriate textboxes with your first name, last name, and email, choose a password to use, select your gender, and enter your birthday (to verify that you are over the age of 13). Then hit the "Sign Up" button.

4. Once you are logged into your new Facebook account, type in our library username, which is _____, in the top search box.

5. Once you see our account you will see a "+1 Add Friend" button at the top of the page. Click that button—You are now friends with us.

If you do not want to sign up to friend us, you can still view the information by going to the site at http://facebook.com/_____. You should either bookmark the site or add it to your favorites list so that you can visit it often because there are new postings daily.

INSTRUCTIONS FOR SETTINSG UP AN EDMODO ACCOUNT

Teacher Signup

1. Go to http://www.edmodo.com.

2. In the middle of the screen you will see the message "Sign Up Now. It's Free!" Under that message choose the "I'm a Teacher" button.

3. Fill in the registration form with a chosen username, chosen password, email address, title, first name, and last name. Check the box that you agree to the "Terms of Service" and click the "Sign Up" button.

4. Locate your school and create an initial group for your classroom. Once you are logged into your account, click the "Create" link in the left column of your homepage.

5. Complete the group registration box by choosing a group name, grade, and subject area. Note the read-only check box below the group name field. If you leave this box unchecked, all group members will be able to post and reply within the group, but if you check it they will only be able to view in read-only mode. Click the "Create" button and you will see a six-digit group code to give students who you want to join your group.

Student Signup

1. Go to http://www.edmodo.com.

2. In the middle of the screen you will see the message "Sign Up Now. It's Free!" Under that message choose the "I'm a Student" button.

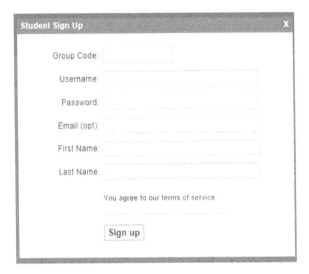

3. Complete the registration form with the code provided by your teacher, a chosen username, a chosen password, and your email address, first name, and last name. Check the box that you agree to the "Terms of Service" and click the "Sign Up" button.

Index

About the Author

DR. MELISSA A. PURCELL is the media specialist at Glynn Academy in Brunswick, Georgia, and is a part-time professor in the instructional technology department at Georgia Southern University. Her media program was recognized as being an Exceptional Media Program for the state of Georgia during the 2009–10 and 2010–11 school years. Her media program was recognized as the Exemplary Media Program for the state of Georgia during the 2011–12 school year. Dr. Purcell was selected as the Library Media Specialist of the Year for Georgia Southeast District in 2007. She is a certified teacher support specialist, is National Board Certified in library media, is Gifted Education endorsed, and has had over 30 articles published in educational journals, books, and newspapers.

www.ingramcontent.com/pod-product-compliance
Lightning Source LLC
Chambersburg PA
CBHW060133060326
40690CB00018B/3861